PHYSICS FOR CLASS 9 (NEW EDITION)

A HAND WRITTEN NOTES

ADITYA RAJ ANAND
SCIENCELAWS.IN

Made with ♥ on the Notion Press Platform
www.notionpress.com

Dedication

To Physics,
The silent poetry of the universe,
The unseen hand that shapes the stars and whispers in the wind.
In every equation, you speak a language deeper than words.
To the laws that govern our reality,
and to the boundless curiosity that propels us to understand.

This book is for you—
For the mysteries you unravel and the wonders you inspire.

Contents

Foreword

About Author

Hello, My name is Aditya Raj Anand an author, digital marketer, blogger, and an entrepreneur. My entrepreneur journey started from 2018 when I completed my schooling. Currently I am doing my bachelor of science in mathematics, after that I have decided to do my Master's in Physics, which I love to demonstrate.

Follow me on instagram @sciencelaws.in If you are science lover you love my containt. You can also ask your doubt in Message box. And You can check my www.sciencelaws.in website and read latetes exam tips and other help.

How i become a digital marketing and web development.

As I told you when I completed my schooling from CBSE, my financial condition was not so good to carry forward my dreams. My dreams was to go in IITs. But unfortunately it was a complete disaster for me to change my path.

But the attachment to the science has not gone by me. So, i decided to start my first blog on science i.e, sciencelaws.in, here I started my passion to demonstrating science in easy language that an Evey student can understand and feel physics, chemistry.

When I was studying, I also feel the problems to understand science. Because science can be understood if it is expressed in easy language.

So, i decided language will not make the problem to understand science for anyone more.

So, I started writing, this book take me a 3 years of publishing. Aslo it was my childhood dream even before the dream of IIT.

Preface

Preface

Physics, as we know, is not just a subject; it is the key to understanding the world around us. From the smallest particles that make up matter to the vastness of the universe, the principles of physics govern everything. With this book, Physics for Class 9, my aim is to make the complexities of this fascinating subject accessible and engaging for young minds.

My name is Aditya Raj Anand, and over the years, I've had the privilege of authoring over five books on physics, helping students and enthusiasts navigate the elegant yet profound concepts that this subject offers. I am also the founder of sciencelaws.in, a personal blog where I share my passion for science, discuss the latest developments, and offer resources to simplify scientific learning.

With an undergraduate degree in Mathematics, I have always been fascinated by the harmony between math and physics. This foundation has allowed me to approach the teaching of physics with a logical and structured mindset, presenting the subject in a way that builds a solid foundation and fosters curiosity.

Physics can sometimes feel overwhelming, especially when students first encounter its fundamental concepts. However, through this book, I hope to guide you through the key principles and encourage you to not just memorize formulas but to deeply understand the "why" and "how" behind them. By the end of this book, I believe you will not only be prepared for your exams but also inspired to see the world through the lens of physics.

This journey through the laws of nature begins here, and I'm honored to be your guide. May this book spark your curiosity and fuel your love for science, as it has done for me throughout my career.

About the Author's Intention Behind Writing This Book

The intention behind writing Physics for Class 9 was simple—to make physics accessible and enjoyable for every student. Over the years, I have noticed how many students often find physics intimidating, not because the subject itself is difficult, but because it's sometimes presented in a way that feels complex or hard to grasp. As someone who has always believed in the beauty of simplicity, my goal with this book is to strip away the technical jargon and bring physics to life in a way that everyone can understand and appreciate.

This book is written in a clear, straightforward, and easy-to-follow language, designed for students who might be hesitant about the subject or struggle with traditional, formula-heavy textbooks. I firmly believe that physics doesn't need to be cloaked in hard language or complicated terms. It's a subject that thrives when presented as a series of simple, logical steps that build upon each other. Every chapter and every concept in this book has been carefully crafted to help you understand the "why" and "how" behind every principle, rather than just memorizing definitions and formulas.

My aim is not to overwhelm you with abstract theory or dense explanations. Instead, I want you to feel confident as you discover the beauty of the physical world around you. Physics is not just about solving problems; it's about seeing the world differently, understanding the forces that shape our reality, and developing critical thinking skills that will stay with you long after your school years.

Whether you're someone who finds traditional textbooks hard to follow or you simply prefer learning through clear and engaging explanations, this book is for you. I hope that as you read, you'll not only grasp the fundamental principles of physics but also come to appreciate the subject as a beautiful, logical, and vital part of the world we live in.

I wrote this book with the intention of making learning physics an enjoyable journey—one that is as simple and rewarding as the subject itself can be.

Aditya Raj Anand

CHAPTER ONE

Unit And Measurement

Unit of Measurement and time

Physics:- The study of nature and natural things.

It is the made of greek word " Fusis" means natural things and nature.

It means that physics is the study of nature and its laws.

Physics is the foundation of engineering and technology.

Physics is based in experiment when experiments are done then it measure with the help of physical quantity.

Quantity means it represents the number.

Physical quantity:- It is represent of the physical laws in the term id quantity.

It is of two types

Scalar quantity and vector quantity.

Scalar quantity means it has only magnitude not direction.

vector quantity means it has both magnitude and as well as direction.

Units

It is of two types

Fundamental unit

Derived unit

Fundamental unit:- It is not depend another unit, three fundamental unit are mass, length and Time.

Derived unit:- It is depend in fundamental unit.

system of unit are four types

Mks system:- In this system Length, Mass and Time are expressed in meter, Kilogram, and Second.

Fps system:- In this system Length, Mass and Time is expressed in Foot, Pound, second.

CGs system:- In this system Length, Mass and Time is expressed in Centimeter, Gram, second.

S.I system;- (international System of Unit) In S.I system having seven fundamental unit.

30 physical quantities with their si units and cgs units

Here is a collection of 30 fundamental and derived physical quantities which commonly used in physics with their si units and CGS units. Also describe the derived quantity with derivation.

We have already discussed about the definition of physical quantity in the above definition. But lets define the physical quantity in another words.

Physical quantity are those quantities which represents the quantities of any material with the help of some symbols attached with numerical values. For example a container contains 6 kilograms of wheat. So we can write 6 kg. Here kg is the physical quantity attached with numerical value of 6.

As we have already seen above that, Physical quantities are two types first is fundamental quantity and second is derived quantity. These are the following 30 physical quantities (both fundamental and derived) with their si units and CGS units. Before we start discussing following 30 physical quantities. Please note that some quantities are derived from fundamental quantity.

30 physical quantities with their si units and cgs units

(1.) Mass (M)

(2.) Distance (S)

(3.) Time (T)

(4.) Speed (s)

(5.) Volume (V)

(6.) Density (D)

(7.) Pressure (P)

(8.) Work (W)

(9.) Energy (E)

(10.) Electric current (A)

(11.) Velocity (V)

(12.) Acceleration (A)

(13.) Displacement (S)

(14.) Force (F)

(15.) torque (τ)

(16.) Electric field (E)

(17.) Angular velocity (ω)

(18.) Linear momentum (P)

(19.) Magnetic dipole moment (?)

(20.) Thrust (T)

(21.) Temperature (T)

(22.) Frequency (μ)

(23.) Amount of substance (Mol)

(24.) Concentration (C)

(25.) Power (P)

(26.) Impulse (I)

(27.) Angle (∠)

(28.) Weight (W)

(29.) Magnetic field (B)

(30.) Gravitation (G)

Lets discuss all of these physical quantities with their definition along with their si and cgs unit.

(1.) Mass (M)

Mass is the scale of measurement of inertia of any body or matter. mass represent the quantity that a body have. greater the mass of a body, less in impact of force in it. mass do not depends on shape and size of a body. that means the greater size of a body need not have a greater mass or vice-versa.

S.I unit of mass:- Kilogram (Kg)
CGS unit of mass:- Gram (g)

(2.) Distance (S)

The actual path covered by the body during the whole journey. It is denoted by S. distance is different from displacement. both have some differences between them. Distance may be in straight line, curved line, or zigzag line. Distance can never be zero untill or unless the body is at rest.

S.I unit of distance:- Meter (m)
CGS unit of distance:- Centimetre (cm)

(3.) Time (T)

Time is an illusion that loses in every second. time is an infinite unfinished continuous events that exist in present, fall in past and will next in future. time is denoted by t.

S.I unit of time:- Second (s)
CGS unit of time:- second (s)

(4.) Speed (s)

Speed is define as the total distance travelled by the body to the total time taken. In other words speed is determined by the distance covered in a specific time period by the body. It is denoted by s.

S.I unit of speed:- meter / sec (m/s)

CGS unit of speed:- centimetre / sec (cm/s)

(5.) Volume (V)

The maximum dimensional area covered by an object in length, breath and height. It is denoted by V. volume is affected by shape and size of a body. means if the body has greater shape and size it may be the body has larger volume or vice-versa.

S.I unit of volume:- meter cube (m3)

CGS unit of volume:- centimetre cube (cm3)

(6.) Density (D)

Density is define as the mass of a body per unit volume. That means if a body has volume 'v' and mass 'm' then density is equal to m/v.

S.I unit density:- kilogram / m2 (kg/m3)

CGS unit density:- gram / cm3 (g /cm3)

(7.) Pressure (P)

Pressure is the force exerted in a unit area of an object. It is denoted by P. pressure is also define as the force per unit area. given by P = F / A.

S.I unit of pressure:- Newton / m2 (N / m2) or Pascal

CGS unit pressure:- Dyne / cm2

(8.) Work (W)

In physics, If a force is applied on a body and the body get displaces from its initial position and covers some distance then work is done. It is denoted by W. work can also be described as the dot product of force and displacement. given by W = F.s.

S.I unit of work:- Joule (N-m) or Newton-meter.

CGS unit of work:- Erg (dyne-cm) or Dyne-centimetre

(9.) Energy (E)

The ability to do some work is called energy. energy can neither be created nor be destroyed but it can be converted into one form to another form. like electric energy into light energy. It is denoted by E.

S.I unit of energy:- Joule

CGS unit of energy:- Erg

(10.) Electric current (A)

It is the flow of electron from one potential to another potential. Flow of electron create potential difference between two points so that electricity generated. It is denoted by A.

S.I unit of electric current:- Ampere

CGS unit of electric current:- Biot

(11.) Velocity (V)

Velocity is define as the distance travelled by the body per unit time in a given direction. Velocity is vector quantity. because it has both magnitude and direction. It is denoted by V. velocity can also be described as the displacement per unit time.

Velocity = Displacement / time

S.I unit of velocity:- meter / sec. (m /s)

CGS unit of velocity:- centimetre / sec. (cm /s)

(12.) Acceleration (A)

Acceleration is the change in velocity with respect to time. In other words, it is the final displacement minus initial displacement whole divided by time. It is denoted by A. Acceleration is vector quantity.

S.I unit of acceleration:- meter / sec2 (m / s2)

CGS unit of acceleration:- centimetre / sec2 (cm / s2)

(13.) Displacement (S)

It is the shortest distance covered by the body in whole journey. In other words, displacement is equal to the distance between initial position and final position of a body. It is denoted by S. Distance may be zero.

S.I unit of displacement:- meter (m)

CGS unit of displacement:- centimetre (cm)

(14.) Force (F)

Force is define as the push or pull of an object is called force. In other words, force is the product of mass and acceleration. It is denoted by F. where F = ma.

S.I unit of force:- Newton (Kg. m /s2)

CGS unit of force:- Dyne (g. cm /s2)

(15.) torque (τ)

It is the measurement of the force acting on a body to determine how much it cause to rotate the body. It is denoted by τ. It is vector quantity.

S.I unit of torque:- Newton-meter (N-m)

CGS unit of torque:- Dyne-centimetre

(16.) Electric field (E)

It is a reason where electric current can be experienced. In other words, electric field is the area where the electric field lines exist. It is denoted by E.

S.I unit of electric field:- Newton / coulomb (volt / meter)

CGS unit of electric field:- Dyne / biot-sec.

(17.) Angular velocity (ω)

Rate of change of angular displacement with respect to time. On other hand angular velocity is how fast the body is moving with respect to time.

S.I unit of angular velocity:- radian / sec

CGS unit of angular velocity:- per second

(18.) Linear momentum (P)

Linear momentum is defined as the product of mass and velocity. It is denoted by P. yhe formula of linear momentum is P = mv. It is vector quantity.

S.I unit of liner momentum:- Kg. m /s

CGS unit of linear momentum:- g. cm /s

(19.) Magnetic dipole moment (?)

Magnetic dipole moment represent the magnetic strength of the magnet with the help of quantity. It is denoted by ?. It is vector quantity because it has both magnitude and direction.

S.I unit of magnetic dipole moment:- weber-meter

CGS unit of magnetic dipole moment:- emu. erg/G

(20.) Thrust (T)

Thrust is the types of force act on upward direction in water.

S.I unit of thrust:- Newton

CGS unit of thrust:- Dyne

(21.) Temperature (T)

It is define as the how hotness and coldness of the body is. It is denoted by T. In other words temperature indicates that how hot or cold a body is.

S.I unit of temperature:- kelvin (k)

CGS unit of temperature:- kelvin

(22.) Frequency (μ)

It is number of cycle of a wave passing in one second. In other words it is cycle per second.

S.I unit of frequency:- Hertz (Hz)

CGS unit of frequency:- Hertz

(23.) Amount of substance (Mol)

Amount of substance is defined as the total number of soute present in total number of solvent.

S.I unit of amount of substance:- Mole

CGS unit of amount of substance:- mole

(24.) Concentration (C)

Concentration is define as the total number of solute or solvent present in a unit volume of solution. In other words it calculate the mass of solute or solvent per unit volume. It is denoted by C.

S.I unit of concentration:- kilogram / m3

CGS unit of concentration:- gram / cm3

(25.) Power (P)

The rate of doing work is called power. power is work per unit time. It is denoted by P.

S.I unit of power:- joule / sec (watt)

CGS unit of power:- erg / sec

(26.) Impulse (I)

Impulse is the force acting for a short period of time.

S.I unit of Impulse:- Newton-second

CGS unit of Impulse:- Dyne-second

(27.) Angle (∠)

It is unitless that expressed in terms of theta.

(28.) Weight (W)

Weight is the force acting in downward direction to the center of the earth. It is the downward force.

S.I unit of weight:- Newton

CGS unit of weight:- Dyne

(29.) Magnetic field (B)

It is the reason where magnetic force is experienced. It is denoted by B.

S.I unit:- Tesla

CGS unit:- oersted

(30.) Gravitation (G)

It the pulling force acting in downward direction toward the center of the planet.

S.I unit:- Newton / kg

CGS unit:- Dyne / g

here you find the actual meaning of scalar and vector quantity. If we define scalar and vector quantity in simple word we can say that scalar quantity are those which have only magnitude not direction, but vector quantity are those which have both magnitude as well as direction. difference between scalar and vector quantity are given below the page for better understanding of these quantities.

1. There are many topics covered in this articles like,
2. What is scalar and vector quantity?
3. List of scalar and vector quantities and their units.
4. Difference between scalar and vector quantity.
5. Product of scalar and vector quantity.

6. What is scalar and vector field?
7. 20 examples of scalar and vector quantity.
8. characteristics of scalar and vector quantities.
9. Types of vector.
10. vector addition and subtraction.
11. What is scalar and vector quantity?

What is scalar and vector quantity?

scalar quantity:- Those quantity which has only magnitude not direction are called scalar quantity.

for example length, mass, speed, work, density, volume etc.

lets understand by taking examples If we say the body have 10 kg of mass it doesn't means not 10 kg of mass in north or south direction.

In other words Those quantity which has only one dimension described by single element like one constant and one variable. for example 5m, 6cm, 2kg, 4mm etc.

Vector quantity:- Those quantity which has both magnitude and a specific direction are called vector quantity.

for example Displacement, Force, acceleration, velocity, torque, momentum etc.

lets understand by taking examples, suppose 2N of force act on the body in North direction, A body is accelerating 5m/s2 in upward direction, Weight (W= mg) of a body acted in the downward direction.

In other word Those quantity which has both two dimension and three dimension described by some more elements like 5m North, 3m/s2, 6m/s, 5N, etc.

Difference between scalar and vector quantity.

These are some differential points on scalars and vectors.

Scalar quantity:-

- Scalar quantity has only magnitude.
- They change if their magnitude change.
- They can be added according to ordinary laws of algebra.

Vector quantity:-

- vectors have both magnitude and direction
- They change if either their magnitude, direction or both change.
- They can be added only by using special laws of vector addition.

Product of scalar and vector quantity

Scalar product and vector product are the two different ways of multiplying two vectors. Multiplication of scalar product has its own rule and Multiplication of vectors product has its own way.

Scalar product (or dot product) of two vectors:- The scalar or dot product of two vectors A and B is defined as the product of the magnitudes of vectors A and B and cosine of the angle θ between them.

vector product (or cross product) of two vectors:- The vector or cross product of two vectors is defined as the vector whose magnitude is equal to the product of the magnitudes of two vectors and sine of the angle between them and whose direction is perpendicular to the plane of the two vectors.

What is scalar and vector field?

A scalar field is something that has a particular value at every point in space. for example temperature at every point on the earth has a particular value but if we move to and fro from that point then the value of temperature will change.

A vector field is just similar to scalar field because vector field also having a value at every point on space. but it has a value and direction at every point in space.

characteristics of scalar and vector quantities.

Before knowing the characteristic of scalar and vector quantities. we have to know hc mcaning of characteristic.

characteristic mcans a quality of something that makes him/her/it different from other people or thing.

so here characteristic of scalar and vector quantity has little same that is magnitude. lets understand it in more detailed.

<u>characteristic of scalar quantities:-</u> scalar quantity has only magnitude. there is no need of direction. speed, distance, time, temperature these all do not need direction.

for example Ramesh played for 3 hours. here we do not need direction.

characteristic of vector quantities:- vector quantities has also magnitude but it needs direction for their illustration. displacement, velocity, acceleration, force etc acquires direction.

for example a body start moving by 3m/s in forward direction. here direction included for better illustration.

Types of vector.

- ***Position vector:-*** A vector which gives position of an object with reference to the origin of a co-ordinate system is called position vector.
- ***Displacement vector:-*** It is that vector which tells how much and in which direction and object has changed its position in a given time interval.
- ***Polar vector:-*** The vector which has a starting point or a point of application are called polar vector.
- ***Axial vector:-*** The vector which represent rotational effect and act along the axis of rotation in right hand screw rule are called axial vector.
- ***Equal vector:-*** Two vectors are said to be equal if they have the same magnitude and same direction.
- ***Negative of a vector:-*** The negative of a vector is defined as another vector having the same magnitude but having an opposite direction.
- ***Modulus of vector:-*** The modulus of a vector means the length or the magnitude of that vector.
- ***Unit vector:-*** A unit vector is a vector of unit magnitude drawn in the direction of a given vector.
- ***Fixed vector:-*** The vector whose initial point is fixed is called a fixed vector.

- ***Zero vector:-*** a zero vector or null vector is a vector that has zero magnitude and an unknown direction.

vector addition and subtraction.

Two vectors can be added or can be subtracted by their rules and laws. vectors can be added by two famous laws

Triangle law of vector addition:- If two vectors can be represented both in magnitude and direction by the two sides of triangle taken in the same order, then their resultant is represented completely, both in magnitude and direction, by the third side of the triangle taken in the opposite order.

Parallelogram law of vector addition:- If two vectors can be represented both in magnitude and direction by the two adjacent sides of a parallelogram drawn from a common point, then their resultant is completely represented, both in magnitude and direction, by the diagonal of the parallelogram passing through the point. see the above picture for more illustration.

Please note that the same rules and theory also use in subtraction of two vectors but you have to replace plus sign from the minus sign.

FAQ on scalar and vector quantities

1. What is scalar and vector quantities?

scalar quantities are those quantities which has only magnitude not direction. speed, time, distance etc.

vector quantities are those quantities which has both magnitude and a specific direction. displacement, velocity, acceleration etc.

2. Is work scalar or vector?

work is scalar quantity which has only magnitude. w= f.s work is dot product of force and displacement. and we know that dot product is scalar quantity.

3. can a scalar be negative?

Yes scalar can be negative. but it depends on situation and types of quantities. like temperature can be negative which is a scalar quantity.

4. Is force a scalar quantity?

No force is a vector quantity. because it has cross product of mass and acceleration. $F= m✖?a \cos\theta$.

5. Where do we use vectors?

vectors can be used in physics to represent physical quantities with direction in the upper head by arrow sign. it is used to represent displacement, velocity, acceleration, etc.

6. Can you square a vector?

No we cannot square a vector because a vector has both magnitude and direction. we can square its magnitude but not direction.

-------------- Team Science laws --------------

CHAPTER TWO

Motion

1. Introduction to Motion

What is Motion?

- Motion is the change in the position of an object with respect to time and its surroundings.
- It involves the object's displacement and the time taken to cover that displacement.

Types of Motion:

- Linear Motion: Motion along a straight line (e.g., a car moving along a straight road).
- Rotational Motion: Motion of an object around a fixed point (e.g., a spinning top).
- Oscillatory Motion: Back-and-forth motion about a central point (e.g., a pendulum).

2. Distance and Displacement

Distance:

- *The total path length covered by an object, regardless of the direction.*
- Scalar quantity (only magnitude, no direction).
- SI unit: meter (m).
- Example: If an object travels 5 m forward and 3 m back, the total distance traveled is 8 m.

Displacement:

- The shortest straight-line distance between the initial and final positions, along with the direction.
- Vector quantity (magnitude and direction).
- SI unit: meter (m).
- Example: If an object moves 5 m east and 3 m west, the displacement is 2 m east.

Difference between Distance and Displacement:

Distance is the total length of the path traveled by an object, regardless of its direction. It is a scalar quantity, meaning it has magnitude but no direction. Distance is always positive and depends on the actual path taken by the object. For example, if you walk 5 meters east and then 5 meters west, the total distance traveled is 10 meters.

Displacement, on the other hand, is the shortest straight-line distance between an object's initial and final positions, along with the direction. It is a vector quantity, meaning it has both magnitude and direction. Displacement can be positive, negative, or zero depending on the relative positions of the start and end points. Using the same example, if you walk 5 meters east and then 5 meters west, the displacement is 0 meters, as you end up at the starting point.

In essence, while distance measures "how much ground an object has covered," displacement measures "how far out of place an object is."

In Short Bullet Points

DISTANCE

- Distance is the total length of the path traveled by an object.
- It is a scalar quantity, meaning it has only magnitude and no direction.
- Distance is always positive and never decreases.
- It depends on the actual path taken by the object.
- The unit of distance in the SI system is the meter (m).
- Distance can never be zero if motion occurs.
- It does not provide information about the direction of motion.
- For a closed path (returning to the start), the distance is the sum of all segments.
- Example: Walking 3 meters forward and 2 meters backward gives a total distance of 5 meters.
- Distance is often used in everyday language to measure the extent of travel.

DISPLACEMENT

- Displacement is the shortest straight-line distance between an object's starting and ending points.
- It is a vector quantity, meaning it has both magnitude and direction.
- Displacement can be positive, negative, or zero.
- It depends only on the initial and final positions, not on the path taken.
- The unit of displacement in the SI system is the meter (m).
- Displacement can be zero even if motion occurs, such as in circular motion.
- It provides information about the direction of motion.
- For a closed path (returning to the start), the displacement is always zero.
- Example: Walking 3 meters forward and 2 meters backward results in a displacement of 1 meter forward.
- Displacement is used in physics to analyze motion and calculate velocity.

Uniform and non uniform motion

Uniform motion is steady and predictable, while non-uniform motion involves changes in speed or direction, making it more complex to analyze.

Uniform Motion Definition

Uniform motion:- When a body moves in such a way that it covers equal distance in equal interval of time however small the time interval may be then speed is said to be uniform motion.

Characteristics:

1. The speed of the object remains constant throughout the motion.
2. The path can be straight or curved, but the rate of motion does not change.
3. Acceleration is zero in uniform motion as there is no change in velocity.
4. It is an idealized concept, often used in physics to simplify calculations.
5. Examples include a car moving at a constant speed of 60 km/h or light traveling in a vacuum.

Graphical Representation:

1. On a distance-time graph, uniform motion appears as a straight line with a constant slope.
2. On a velocity-time graph, the motion is represented as a horizontal line.

Non Uniform Motion Definition

Non uniform motion:- if body travels equal distance in unequal interval of time/ unequal distance cover in equal interval of time then it is called non uniform motion.

Characteristics:

1. The speed of the object varies over time.
2. The motion can involve acceleration or deceleration.
3. Acceleration is non-zero and may change direction.
4. Non-uniform motion is more common in real-life scenarios.
5. Examples include a car slowing down at a red light, a ball rolling down a hill, or a rocket ascending.

Graphical Representation:

1. On a distance-time graph, non-uniform motion appears as a curved line.
2. On a velocity-time graph, it is represented by a sloping or irregular curve.

What is Speed?

- The distance traveled by a body per unit time over a short interval of time is called its speed.
- S.I unit of speed is m/s.
- C.Gs unit of speed is cm/s.
- speed is the scalar quantity.

What is Velocity?

- The displacement covered by a body per unit time is called velocity.
- S.I unit of velocity is m/s.
- C.Gs unit is cm/s.
- velocity is vector quantity it has both magnitude and direction.

What is Average speed?

- It is the ratio of total distance traveled by total time taken.
- It is a scalar quantity.
- It's S.I unit is m/s.
- It is denoted by 'V' .

What is Acceleration?

- Rate of change of velocity with respect to time.
- Acceleration = final velocity - initial velocity/ time
- $a = v - u / t$
- S.I unit of acceleration is m/s2.
- Acceleration may be positive, Negative or Zero.

Acceleration are two types

<u>Uniform Acceleration:-</u>

When a body travels in a straight lines and its velocity changes by equal amounts is equal interval of time then it is called Uniform acceleration.

<u>Non uniform Acceleration:-</u>

When the velocity of a body changes by unequal amount in equal interval of time then it is called non uniform acceleration.

Positive acceleration is simply called acceleration.

Negative acceleration is simply called Retardation.

Three equation of motion

These equations are valid only for motion under constant acceleration. They are fundamental tools in kinematics and are widely used to solve problems in mechanics.

1. First equation of motion

The first equation of motion is a mathematical expression that relates the final velocity (vv) of an object to its initial velocity (uu), acceleration (aa), and the time (tt) for which the object has been in motion.

<u>Definition:</u>

The first equation of motion, v=u+atv = u + at, states that the final velocity of an object is equal to its initial velocity plus the product of acceleration and time.

Key Points:

- It is used to calculate the velocity of an object after a certain time when it is undergoing constant acceleration.
- This equation assumes uniform acceleration.
- Each term in the equation has a physical significance:
- vv: The velocity of the object at the end of time tt.

- uu: The velocity of the object at the start of motion.
- aa: The rate of change of velocity (acceleration).
- t: The time duration of motion.

This equation is fundamental in understanding linear motion and is widely applied in physics problems involving kinematics.

Mathematically, Its like that

$V = u + at$

Proof :- we know that

acceleration = change in velocity/ time taken

$a = v - u/t$

$at = v - u$

$at + u = v$

or

$v = u + at$

Where,

V = final velocity

U = initial velocity

T = time

A = acceleration

2. *Second equation of motion*

The second equation of motion describes the displacement (ss) of an object in terms of its initial velocity (uu), acceleration (aa), and the time (tt) it has been in motion.

It is mathematically expressed as:

s=ut+1/2at2

s = ut + {1}/{2}at^2

Key Points:

- Displacement (ss): The distance covered by the object along its path during motion.
- This equation is used to calculate the displacement of an object moving under uniform acceleration over a certain time (tt).
- Each term in the equation has a specific physical meaning:
- ut: The displacement due to the object's initial velocity.
- 1/2at^2: The additional displacement caused by the object's acceleration.

Assumptions:

- The object moves with constant acceleration.
- The motion is along a straight line.

Applications:

- To find how far an object has traveled during a given time.
- To analyze motion in scenarios like a freely falling object or a car accelerating on a straight road.

Mathematically, its Like that

S = ut + 1/2 at2

Proof

Average speed = u + v/2

Distance = Average speed * time

S =(u + v/2)* t

We know that

v = u + at

put value of v

S = ut + ut + at2/ 2

= 2 ut + at^2/ 2
S = ut + 1/2 at2

3. Third equation of motion

The third equation of motion relates the final velocity (vv) of an object, its initial velocity (uu), the acceleration (aa), and the displacement (ss) traveled, without involving time (tt).

It is mathematically expressed as:
v2=u2+2as

Key Points:

- Final velocity (vv): The velocity of the object at the end of the motion.
- Initial velocity (uu): The velocity of the object at the start of the motion.
- Acceleration (aa): The rate of change of velocity.
- Displacement (ss): The distance the object has traveled in the direction of the acceleration.

Explanation:

This equation is useful when time (tt) is not given, but the displacement, initial velocity, acceleration, and final velocity are known or need to be calculated. It expresses the relationship between velocity and displacement for uniformly accelerated motion.

Applications:

- To calculate the final velocity of an object without needing the time variable.

- Used in problems involving objects with constant acceleration, such as freely falling bodies or vehicles accelerating on a road.

Mathematically, Its like That

$v2 = u2 + 2as$

We know that,

$V = u + at$

and ,

$S = ut + 1/2\ at2$

From $V = u + at$

$t = v - u/a$

$S = ut + 1/2\ at2$

$S = u*(\ v - u/a) + 1/2 * a *(\ v - u/a\ )2$

$2as + u2 = v2$

$v2 = u2 + 2as$

------------- Team Science laws --------------

CHAPTER THREE

Force And Laws Of Motion

Force and Laws of Motion

Force :- It may be defined as push or pull which produces (tends to produces) a change in the state of rest or uniform motion of a body or change in the direction of motion of the body.

Force may also change the Shape of the body or produces rotational effect.

Force is a vector quantity because Force have as well as magnitude and direction.

The non-living body also exert a Force.

Example:- (i) When we suspended a heavy block From a rope. The rope holds the block just as a man can hold in the air.

(ii) When a cork is dipped in Water it comes to the surface due to the upward. Force exerted by water.

Force (Detailed Definition):

Force is a physical quantity that can cause an object to undergo a change in its state of motion, shape, or direction. It is a vector quantity, meaning it has both magnitude and direction. When a force acts on an object, it can result in an acceleration (change in velocity), deformation, or a change in the object's direction.

Characteristics of Force:

Vector Quantity:

Force has both magnitude (how much force) and direction (which way the force is applied).

It can be represented as an arrow, where the length of the arrow indicates the magnitude and the direction of the arrow shows the direction of the force.

SI Unit:

The SI unit of force is the Newton (N), named after Sir Isaac Newton.

1 Newton(N)=1 kg·1m/s2

This means that a force of 1 N will accelerate a 1 kg mass by 1 m/s2.

Representation:

Force is commonly represented by the symbol F.

It can be calculated using Newton's Second Law of Motion: F=m·aF = m \cdot a where mm is the mass of the object, and aa is the acceleration produced.

Types of Force:

1. Contact Forces: These forces act when two objects are in physical contact with each other. Examples include:

2. Friction: The force that resists motion between two surfaces in contact.
3. Tension: The force exerted by a string, rope, or cable when pulled.
4. Normal Force: The support force exerted by a surface to support the weight of an object resting on it.
5. Applied Force: A force applied by a person or another object.
6. Non-contact Forces:
7. These forces act without physical contact between the objects. Examples include:
8. Gravitational Force: The force of attraction between two objects due to their mass. For example, Earth attracts objects toward its center, causing objects to fall.
9. Electrostatic Force: The force exerted by electrically charged particles on one another.
10. Magnetic Force: The force exerted by magnets on materials or other magnets.

Effects of Force:

- Change in Motion: Force can alter the velocity of an object (speed up, slow down, or change direction). This is the basis of Newton's Second Law.
- Change in Shape: Force can deform an object. For example, applying pressure can compress a spring or bend a piece of metal.
- Equilibrium: If forces are balanced (net force = 0), the object will either remain at rest or continue moving with constant velocity.

Examples of Force:

Push or Pull: A force exerted by applying a push (e.g., pushing a door open) or a pull (e.g., pulling a cart).

Gravitational Force: The force that causes objects to fall towards the Earth when dropped.

Magnetic Force: A magnet attracting a metal object.

In Summary:

Force is a fundamental concept in physics that explains how objects interact and move. It is central to the understanding of dynamics and is essential in analyzing any kind of motion, whether it's the motion of planets, cars, or even microscopic particles.

Galileo's Experiment: (Aristotle)

(iii) When we comb our der hair and bring the comb close to bits of paper the piece jumps to the comb therefore, we can say the Force is interaction between two bodies.

A Greek philosopher give the idea that a constant Force is needed to keep a body moving with constant velocity it means that if a constant Force not applied the body will come to rest. Thus, the natural state of a body is that of rest.

In 17th century Galileo Galilei and Italian scientist opposed the idea of Aristotle according to Galileo no Force was needed to keep a body in constant velocity it means that natural state of a body it is oppose the change in its of motion.

Newton's 1st law of motion

Every object continuous in a state of rest or of uniform motion in a straight line if external force no applied on the body.

'Inertia' this term is well known for those who take interest in physics. Inertia is a very important part of physics. But our question is from where this inertia came. So a quite simple answer would be from "Newton's laws of motion". So in this post we will not only discuss the types of inertia and their examples but also we will try to find out how inertia originated from Newton's law.

A famous person said that there are total 10% physics covered if you know Newton's laws. Here Newton's laws means not only three laws but all the portions including inertia, momentum, etc.

Now, let's focus on our main topic that is inertia of rest. So before we start the definition of Inertia. Let's understand what we have to know to understand full concept of inertia of rest.

So these are the things and terms related to inertia that everyone should know to clear the full concept of inertia of rest.

1. What is inertia?
2. Types of inertia?
3. What is inertia of rest?
4. Inertia of rest in terms of Newton's law.
5. Deep discussion on inertia of rest.
6. Property of inertia of rest.
7. Factors depends on inertia of rest.
8. One experiment to demonstrate inertia of rest.
9. Eight most common examples of inertia of rest in our daily life.

What is inertia?

We have studied in our previous classes that inertia is the tendency of a body to remain it in their original state. No matter whether the body is moving or stop.

In more simple way we can say that inertia is the legacy or identity of any object. Means that inertia indicates or tells about the nature of a body. But is that's it about inertia? Is there this limited information available about inertia?

We can't say anything because in our childhood we have just studied that much. So it's time to know more about inertia.

Apart from the types of inertia that we will discuss later in this post. Let's take a deep breath and lost on the deep analysis of inertia.

Everything in this universe is in two forms whether it may be in position of rest or in motion. Those bodies which are in a state of raised in this universe may because of some universal force or gravity. And those bodies which are in a state of motion may because of the some same universal force of gravity.

So how we can say that there has the body's tendency to remains at in state of rest or in state of motion. If something is in a state of rest may be because some force act on it. For example let's suppose a football is placed in playground. Now here two situation arises.

Situation No 1 :-

The football on the ground is at in a state of rest may because no one applied an external force on it.

Situation No 2 :-

The football on the ground is at in state of rest may because of the flat surface with gravity pulling. If the ground will be incline it will start moving with gravity force.

No from the above discussion on two situation. We have understood that inertia of anybody it is not only sustainable with external force. But also unbalanced force.

Hence, in the definition of inertia we have to say that inertia is the tendency of a body to remains its state of rest or uniform motion until or unless no any external or unbalanced force applied on it.

Let's understand the concept of unbalanced force in Inertia.

As we have discussed above about two situation. The first is about no external force applied on the rest football. And the second is gravity. So here in this case of rest football on the ground. The gravitational force has cancelled by upward Normal force. Hence the resultant force will be zero. Therefore, the football has a tendency of rest called football has inertia.

Types of Inertia

According to Newton's first law of motion. The inertia can be divided into three parts.

1. Inertia of rest.
2. Inertia of motion.
3. Inertia of direction.

Today in this post we will only discuss about inertia of rest. Not only the definition but also the top 8 examples of inertia of rest that we have seen in our daily life.

All the scientific phenomenon whether it inertia, Newton's laws, thermodynamics laws, gravitation etc can be seen in our daily life style. We have to just open our scientific mind of seen.

As similar to other phenomenon that happen in our daily life. The one most common is inertia of rest. So before we discuss the examples of inertia of rest. Let's take an overview about what is inertia of rest?

What is inertia of rest in simple words

Inertia of rest is simply defined as the tendency of any body to remains the original state of rest is called Inertia of rest.

In other words, if a body is in position of rest means it is not moving from one place to another then we can say that the body has a tendency to remains in state of rest.

Inertia of rest in terms of Newton's law

The concept of inertia of rest, inertia of motion and inertia of direction comes from Newton's first law of motion.

According to Newton's first law of motion those bodies which are in state of rest remains in rest or in motion remains in motion until or unless no external or unbalanced force applied on it.

The definition is quite similar to the definition of inertia because the concept of Newton's first law and inertia is same.

Inertia is originated from Newton's first law. You can also say that inertia is the refined concept of Newton's first law.

Deep discussion on Inertia of rest

Newton discovered three laws. Galileo was the first who talked about laws of motion and gravitation. But after the death of Galileo, it was Newton who published the three laws of motion called Newton's laws of motion. After the discovery of Newton's first law, the concept of inertia came.

Now, the question is why the concept of inertia came from Newton's first law. So the answer is hidden in the definition of Newton's first law.

As we know, Newton's first law says that any body which have a state of rest to remains in rest or which have a state of motion it also remains in motion. For example if a body is moving, it doesn't means some force is responsible for moving that body. It is the tendency of that body to keep moving forever until or unless no external or unbalanced force applied to it.

As we know the definition of inertia of rest is extracted from Newton's first law. Now, the meaning of inertia is also quite similar to the meaning of mass. That means if a body has some masses, then it has also some inertia.

So we can say that inertia is a type of force that can be experienced when the state of body changes. For example if we sit in a bus which is in rest. And if the bus suddenly start moving we will experience some backward force because of inertia of rest. Hence, we conclude that inertia is also a type of force.

Property of inertia of rest

These are some properties that describe the inertia of rest.

The first property of inertia of rest of a body is that it resist the change in their state of motion.

The second property of inertia of rest of a body is that some forces are necessary to apply to move the rest body.

The last property is that when a body is at rest. It has a definite amount of inertia due to certain mass of the body.

Factors depends on inertia of rest

There are two simple factors that the inertia of rest of a body depends.

The first factors that affect Inertia of rest is mass of a body. Means more the masses of a body. More will be inertia and less will be mass the less will be inertia.

The second factors that affect Inertia of rest is density of a body. More will be density the higher will be inertia and vice versa.

One experiment to demonstrate inertia of rest

To perform this experiment take one glass, one square playing card and one 5 rupees coin.

Now, we have all the things that is necessary to perform the experiment of inertia of rest. We will perform this experiment in five simple steps. So let's start.

Step 1 :- Take one 5 rupees coin, one square size playing card and one glass.

Step 2 :- Now, placed this card on the above of the glass filled with water.

Step 3 :- After placing the card, let's place teh coin above the card.

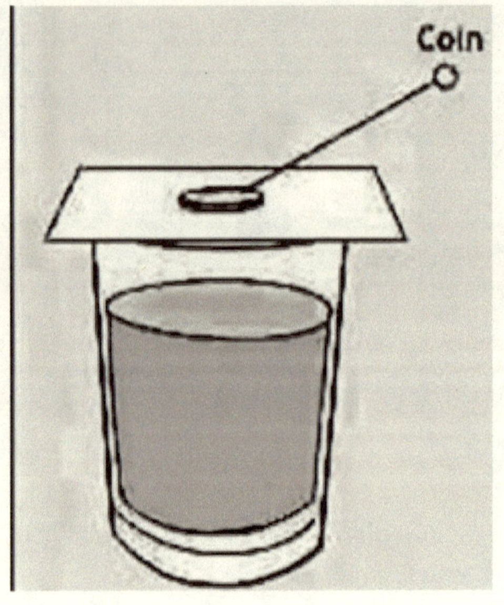

Step 4 :- Pull the playing card suddenly in backward direction.

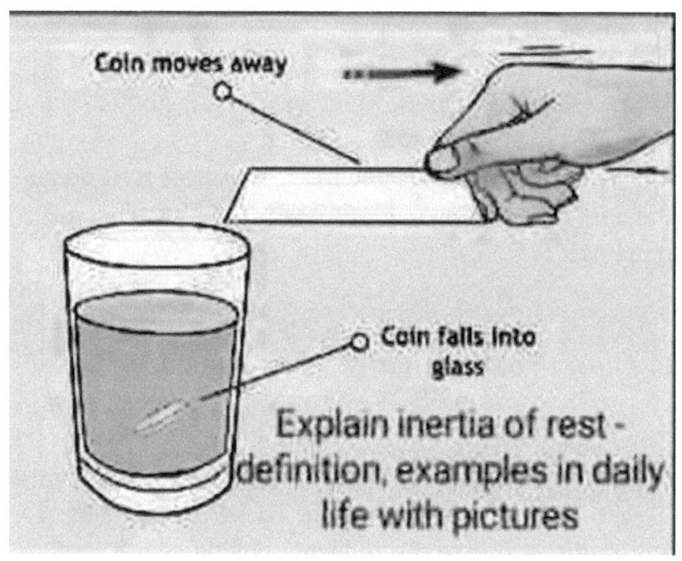

Step 5 :- After pulling it in inward direction the coin falls down vertically in the glass. This is because the original state of the coin was at rest. But after suddenly pulling the card. The card Start moving in backward direction. But card has a tendency to remains its state of rest. So it falls down vertically. This shows that the coin follows the concept of inertia of rest.

8 most common examples of inertia of rest in our daily life.

Here are the 8 examples of inertia of rest with explanation that we experiences in our day to day life.

1. Felling jerk after bus start moving.

This happens as follows, when we sat on a stop bus and if the bus start moving suddenly then we feel a background jerk in our body. This is due to the inertia of rest. Because the bus get motion but our body has the tendency to remains it in state of rest.

2. Coin drop vertically when the card flick.

Now, take a playing card, a coin and a glass of water. Put the card on the top of the glass and put coin on the card. Now, flick or pull the card in the backward direction. You will find that due to the suddenly pulling of the card, the coin drop into the glass filled with water.

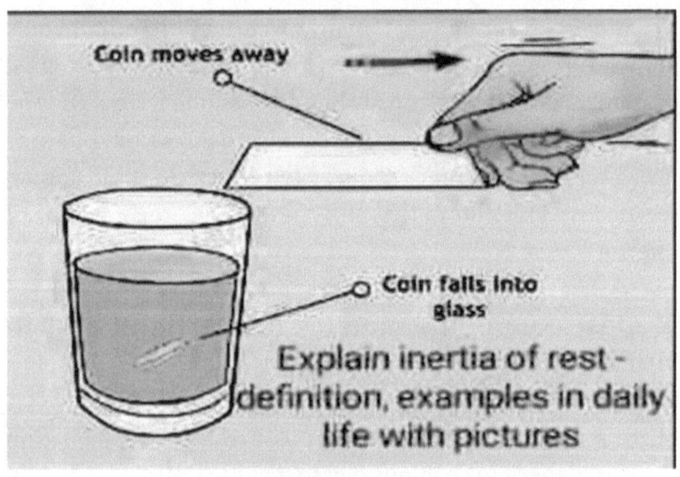

This happen as follows When we put coin and card on the glass. All these things was in state of rest. But after the we have pulled the card, we applied a force only on the card not the coin placed above the card. So due to the tendency of the coin to remains in original state i.e, rest. The coin falls vertically into the glass.

3. Dust appear after shaking of dirty clothes.

You have must seen that when we beat the dirty clothes or blankets with sticks. Or even if we shake dirty clothes with our hands in sunlight. The dust particles appears to moving in surrounding of clothes. Have you ever be think, why this happens. So this happens because of inertia of rest of dust particles.

This happens as follows, when we start beating the dirty clothes. The the cloth start moving in to and fro motion but the dust particles remains in state of rest. So due to not moving of dust particles with cloth it seems like moving in surrounding.

4. Bullet makes a fine hole in glass

This example is very interesting. You have seen in many movies that when a person shoots a glass door with gun. The bullet of the gun makes a fine hole to the size of the bullet without breaking the glass.

This happens as follows : initially the glass of the window are in rest. But after the gun fired. The bullet strikes with the glass in a perticular are with respect to the size of the bullet. And dur to the very high speed of the bullet. The glass piece from that area where the bullet strikes goes with the bullet and makes a fine hole.

5. Glass not falls after table cloth removed.

Many magician performed this magic in different different show. You have must seen that magic.

Let's perform that magic. Take a glass of water. Placed it on the table with table cloth.

Now, pull the table clothes with high force. You will notice that the glass filled with water not drop. Even their water. So how this happens.

This happens as : when we suddenly pull the table clothes. The cloth get a motion and leave the tendency of rest. But the water glass was still in state of rest. Hence, due to the inertia of rest the glass not falls down after the cloth removed from the table.

6. Falling of fruits after shaking tree.

When we shake guava, or mango tree. The fruits fall down because the fruits wants to remains in state of rest.

7. Moved backward when train start from station.

When train start moving. The wheal of the train gets motion but the passenger has a tendency to remains in state of rest. Hence, it experienced a jerk in backward direction.

8. Shutter feels heavy during shop close.

If you noticed that when we pull the shutter to close the shop. The shutter feels quite heavy. This is due to the two reasons. First is due to their high mass and other is due to inertia of rest.

Before we apply a pulling force to the shop Shutter. The shutter is in state of rest. Even after applying force the shutter wants to remains at in state of rest. Hence, we feels heavy during shop close.

After a long discussion on Inertia of rest. The time has come to talk about inertia of motion. Not only the definition but also 10 examples of inertia of motion that we have all experienced in our day to day life.

Deep Discussion On Inertia Of Motion

After a long discussion on Inertia of rest. The time has come to talk about inertia of motion. Not only the definition but also 10 examples of inertia of motion that we have all experienced in our day to day life.

But before we go further, let's make a table of contents for this post.

Topic covered in this lecture

- What is an Inertia of motion?
- Formula of inertia of motion.

Q. What is inertia give an example of inertia of motion also explain which of the following has more inertia an empty box or a box full of books?

- Daily life examples of inertia of motion with visual picture.
- Application of inertia of motion.
- Where is Inertia of motion came from?
- Why inertia of motion related to Newton's first law of motion?

All the above topic are well explained in the following notes. So let's start.

What is inertia of motion?

If we talk about only inertia, neither rest nor motion. Then it is a tendency of a body to keep their original state.

So, Inertia of motion is defined as the tendency of a body to keep their original state of motion forever. Untill or unless an external force is applied to it.

Please note that :- In inertia of motion, the direction of the moving object also constant. Means will be moving in only one direction forever.

Let's take an example to understand the inertia of motion more clearly.

Case 1:-

Suppose a car is running on a straight road at a speed of 40 km/h. After 5 hours of constant moving, a curve turning has come. Now, if we didn't apply the external force (or brake) the car will be accident.

But if we apply the brake to the car, suddenly we feel a forward jerk. This jerk is because of inertia of motion.

This explains as follows : When we apply the brake the car has stopped but our body has a tendency to keep their original state of motion. Due to this we feel jerk in the forward direction.

Case 2:-

Suppose the same car is running on a straight road at a speed of 40 km/h. After 3 hours of constant moving a road breaker has come.

Now, when the car cross the breaker, the wheel of the car leave the ground for some minor second and after that it again touches the ground. But due to this we felt a jump inside the car.

This jump is because of inertia of motion. This explains as follows:

While the constant moving of the car. Our body is in state of rest with respect to other person inside the car. But in motion with respect to the people who has seen from outside the car.

Please note that :- This case is also a good example of rest and motion are relative terms.

So, after crossing the road breaker our body gain some motion but after some micro second it again touches the ground. So we felt jump in upward direction.

Case 3:-

Suppose, we are sitting in the same car. After some time, if we change the direction of the car. We felt down in the right side because of the inertia of direction.

Rest and motion are relative terms.

Suppose a person is standing on the moon. We can say that person is in state of rest with respect to another person stand beside them. But in motion with respect to that person who seen both of them from earth.

Let's take another example to illustrate our above example.

Suppose we are sitting on a running train. Here we can say that we are in state of rest with respect to other passages sitting besides us. But we are still in motion with respect to the passages standing on the platform.

formula of inertia of motion

- Please note that there is no definite formula to calculate the inertia of motion, rest or direction.
- Inertia is a phenomenon in science. It is not a mathematical concepts or equations.
- The inertia of momentum has a formula. But not inertia of motion.
- Inertia of motion is used to understand the concept of the questions. Inertia can be used to clean the concept of Newton's first law of motion.

Q. What is inertia give an example of inertia of motion also explain which of the following has more inertia an empty box or a box full of books?

In most simple words, Inertia is the tendency or behaviour of a body that helps them to keep their original state unless or until an external force is applied to it.

Please not that the body may be in state of rest or motion.

Example of inertia of motion.

Applying brake suddenly when the car is in motion. This explains as follows:

When the car is moving in a straight line at constant speed. And if we apply the brake, it goes slow down and Stop after some time. Due to the inertia of motion. Because the moving car always wants to remains in motion as according to Newton's first law. But when we apply brake, Newton's law break. That's the reason we feel forward force after applying brake.

Now, the question is which has more inertia.

1. An empty box.
2. A box with full of books.

Hence, to answer this question. Let's first understand that the object which has more masses has more inertia than the lighter one.

So, here the box full of books has more inertia than the empty box.

Daily life examples of inertia of motion with visual picture

1. Feel backward force when car suddenly start.
2. Feel forward force when car suddenly stops.
3. Collision of moving objects in space.
4. Moving of satellite in space.
5. Moving of planets in space.
6. Jump from moving train.
7. Objects come to you when throw inside the moving train.
8. Athletes not stop running even after reach to the final position.
9. The moving of bike for some time, even we off the engine.
10. Continuous moving of stone attached with thread in circular path.

These are the 10 most common and familiar examples of inertia of motion that we have expressed in our life.

1. Feel backward force when car suddenly start.

When a car suddenly starts, you feel a backward force because of inertia, which is a property of matter described by Newton's First Law of Motion. Here's an explanation of why this happens:

Inertia is the tendency of an object to resist changes in its state of motion. According to Newton's First Law, an object at rest will stay at rest, and an object in motion will stay in motion unless acted upon by an external force.

When you are sitting in the car at rest and the car suddenly accelerates forward:

The car starts moving forward, but your body, which was initially at rest, tends to stay in the same position because of inertia.

To compensate for the sudden acceleration, your body resists the forward motion, which causes you to feel as if you're being pushed backward relative to the car.

2.Feel forward force when car suddenly stops.

When a car suddenly stops, you feel a forward force due to inertia, which is a consequence of Newton's First Law of Motion. Here's why this happens:

When the car suddenly stops:

The car decelerates (slows down) quickly, but your body, which was moving forward with the car, wants to keep moving at the same speed because of its inertia.

Since your body tends to keep moving forward while the car is now decelerating, you feel as if you are being pushed forward.

Understanding the Force

As the car comes to a sudden stop, it exerts a backward force on you (via the seat and seatbelt).

Your body resists the sudden deceleration and wants to continue moving forward.

The forward force you feel is your body's resistance to this change in motion. Essentially, you're trying to maintain the forward velocity that you had before the car stopped, and this results in the sensation of being pushed forward.

This is why you feel like you're being pushed forward when the car suddenly stops. The seatbelt or any other restraint system in the car works to counteract this forward motion by applying a backward force to bring your body to a stop along with the car.

3. Collision of moving objects in space.

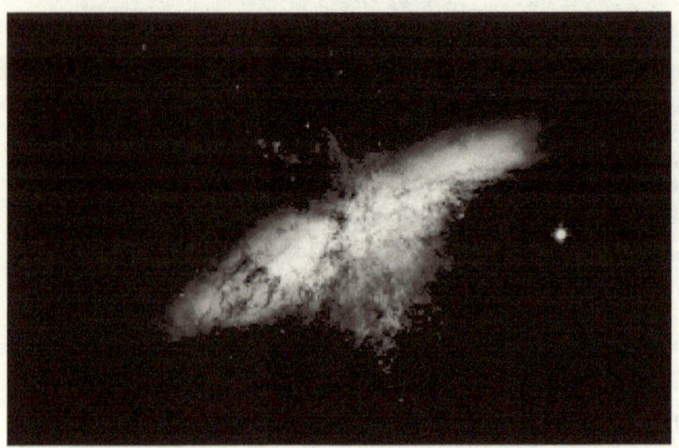

Collisions between moving objects in space can occur in a variety of scenarios, such as the collision of asteroids, comets, spacecraft, or even smaller particles like space debris. These collisions are governed by the basic principles of physics, including **momentum conservation, energy conservation**, and the **laws of motion**.

Key Concepts in Collisions of Moving Objects in Space:

1. **Conservation of Momentum**: In an isolated system, where no external forces are acting, the total momentum before the collision is equal to the total momentum after the collision. This is a fundamental principle known as **conservation of momentum**.

Momentum (pp) is the product of an object's mass and its velocity (p=mvp = mv).

- If two objects collide in space, their combined momentum before and after the collision remains the same, assuming no external forces (like gravity or friction) are involved during the brief time of the collision.

2. **Conservation of Energy**: In the case of **elastic collisions**, both kinetic energy and momentum are conserved. However, in **inelastic collisions**, while momentum is conserved, some of the kinetic energy is transformed into other forms of energy, such as heat, sound, or deformation (like crumpling in the case of spacecraft).

    - In space, the lack of air resistance means that energy lost as heat or sound might not dissipate in the same way as on Earth, but energy still gets converted into other forms (e.g., deformation of objects or the production of heat).

3. **Types of Collisions**:

    - **Elastic Collision**: Both momentum and kinetic energy are conserved. After the collision, the objects bounce off each other without any permanent deformation. This is a rare occurrence in space since most space objects are not perfectly rigid.
    - **Inelastic Collision**: Momentum is conserved, but kinetic energy is not. Some energy is lost, and the objects may deform or break apart. For example,

when two asteroids collide, they might break into fragments, and the fragments might continue to move with the combined momentum of the original objects.

- **Perfectly Inelastic Collision**: This is the extreme case where the colliding objects stick together after the collision, moving as one mass with the combined momentum. This type of collision is also common when large objects like asteroids collide, often resulting in the formation of a new, single object.

4. **Force of Impact**: The force experienced during a collision depends on the change in momentum and the duration of the collision. In space, objects like asteroids or comets have extremely high velocities, so even a seemingly small change in velocity can result in a significant release of energy.
5. **Relativistic Effects**: In high-speed collisions (i.e., when objects approach significant fractions of the speed of light), relativistic effects become important. In such cases, both momentum and energy must be considered in the relativistic form, which takes into account the increase in mass as an object approaches the speed of light.

Example: Collision of Asteroids in Space

- Suppose two asteroids are on a collision course, moving at velocities v1 and v2, and have masses m1 and m2, respectively. The total momentum before the collision would be:

total=m1v1+m2v2

After the collision, if the asteroids collide elastically, the velocities change, but the total momentum remains the same. However, if the collision is inelastic, the kinetic energy will be partially converted into other forms of energy, such as heat or deformation.

Outcome of Collisions in Space

- **Creation of Craters**: The collision of large objects (like asteroids) can create craters on planets or moons, as seen in Earth's history with the impact that contributed to the extinction of the dinosaurs.
- **Fragments and Debris**: If objects collide with high velocity, they may break into smaller fragments. These fragments could continue to move through space, potentially causing further collisions.
- **Spacecraft Collisions**: In the case of spacecraft, a collision could be catastrophic. Spacecraft and satellites often take precautions to avoid collisions with space debris, which can cause significant damage at high speeds, despite the lack of atmosphere in space.

Conclusion

Collisions in space, although occurring in the vacuum of space where there is no air resistance, still obey fundamental physical laws, particularly the conservation of momentum and energy. The outcomes of these collisions depend on the types of objects involved, their velocities, and the nature of the collision. The lack of atmospheric drag means that objects continue moving with high velocities post-collision, which could lead to lasting effects like fragmentation or the creation of new objects.

4. Moving of satellite in space.

Satellites in space move according to the principles of orbital mechanics, primarily governed by the gravitational force and centripetal force. Here's an explanation of how satellites move in space:

1. Orbital Motion and Gravitational Force

A satellite in orbit around a planet or other celestial body is essentially in free fall, constantly being pulled toward the planet by gravity. However, its tangential velocity (speed in a direction perpendicular to the force of gravity) keeps it from falling directly to the surface.

The gravitational force between the planet and the satellite provides the centripetal force that keeps the satellite in orbit.

Inertia causes the satellite to move in a straight line unless acted upon by an external force, while gravity continually pulls the satellite toward the planet, creating a curved path. This balance of forces results in the satellite continuously "falling" around the planet, maintaining its orbit.

5. Moving of planets in space.

Inertia: According to Newton's First Law of Motion, an object in motion tends to remain in motion at a constant velocity unless acted upon by an external force. In the case of a planet, its inertia wants it to move in a straight line, but the Sun's gravitational pull prevents it from flying off into space.

Thus, planets move in orbits, constantly falling towards the Sun due to gravity, but their inertia causes them to keep moving forward, creating an elliptical orbit.

6. Jump from moving train.

Jumping from a moving train is extremely dangerous and should be avoided at all costs. However, understanding the physics behind it helps explain why it's so risky. Here's what happens:

When you're inside a moving train, you are moving at the same speed as the train, relative to the ground outside. If the train is moving at 50 km/h, you, along with everything inside, are also moving at 50 km/h in the same direction as the train.

Relative to the train: You are stationary in the train.

Relative to the ground: You are moving at the same speed as the train.

When you jump off the train, your body still retains the horizontal speed of the train (50 km/h, for example) at the moment you leave it, since there is no external force to stop that horizontal motion immediately.

What Happens When You Jump Off : At the moment you jump, you maintain the horizontal velocity of the train. This means that even after leaving the train, you will still be moving forward at the same speed as the train (unless air resistance or friction acts on you).

7. Objects come to you when throw inside the moving train.

In a moving train, if you throw an object backward, it might appear to come toward you relative to your position inside the train, because you and the object are both moving forward at the same speed as the train. However, relative to the ground outside, the object retains the train's speed (forward or backward), and its motion is adjusted accordingly.

When you throw an object inside a moving train, the behavior of the object depends on the relative motion between you, the train, and the object.

8. Athletes not stop running even after reach to the final position.

Athletes continue running even after reaching the finish line due to their inertia, momentum, and the need for gradual deceleration to avoid injury. The combination of physiological and psychological factors means that it takes a moment for them to stop, even after they've crossed the final position in a race.

When athletes run in a race and continue running even after reaching the final position, it's due to several factors related to inertia, momentum, and reaction to the environment. Here's an explanation of why this happens:

Inertia and Momentum :-

Inertia is the tendency of an object to resist changes in its motion. According to Newton's First Law of Motion, an object in motion will stay in motion unless acted upon by an external force.

When an athlete is running at high speed, they have momentum — the product of their mass and velocity. Even if they reach the finish line, their body will want to continue moving due to inertia, which means they will keep running for a brief moment after crossing the finish line.

9. The moving of bike for some time, even we off the engine.

When a bike continues to move for some time even after the engine is turned off, it is due to the concept of inertia and the momentum of the bike. Here's an explanation of what happens:

Inertia and Momentum :- Inertia: According to Newton's First Law of Motion, an object in motion will remain in motion unless acted upon by an external force. In the case of the bike, the inertia of the bike's motion makes it continue moving even after the engine is turned off.

Momentum: The bike has momentum — the product of its mass and velocity. When the engine is running, the bike gains momentum as it moves forward. Even after you turn off the engine, the bike retains this momentum and will continue moving forward for a while until external forces (like friction, air resistance, and the brakes) slow it down.

10. Continuous moving of stone attached with thread in circular path.

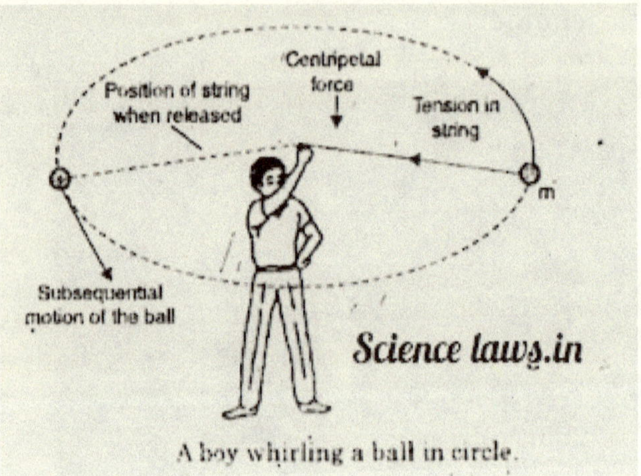

A boy whirling a ball in circle.

Inertia of the Stone :- The stone has inertia, which is its tendency to resist changes in motion. If there were no force acting on it, the stone would move in a straight line tangent to the circular path at any point.

However, because the thread pulls the stone toward the center, it prevents the stone from flying off in a straight line. The result is that the stone moves in a circular path instead.

Application of inertia of motion.

- Application of car brakes, train brakes etc works on the inertia of motion.
- The runner athelete also uses the application of inertia of motion for long jumping.
- The scientist also uses the application of inertia of motion in space satellite.
- The study of the motion of earth and other planets can be understood by the application inertia of motion.
- Aeroplane take off and landing is also use application of inertia of motion.

Why inertia of motion related to Newton's first law

According to Newton's first law of motion, a rest body always remains in state of rest and a moving object always in state of motion.

Hence, inertia of motion said that, a body which is moving with some velocity. It always moving forever until or unless an external force is applied to it.

So, the definition of both the term are inter relative. Not only the definition but also the concept of both the terms are co-related.

Application of inertia of motion

Application of car brakes, train brakes etc works on the inertia of motion.

The runner athelete also uses the application of inertia of motion for long jumping.

The scientist also uses the application of inertia of motion in space satellite.

The study of the motion of earth and other planets can be understood by the application inertia of motion.

Aeroplane take off and landing is also use application of inertia of motion.

Linear momentum

It is measured by the products of the mass of the particle and its velocity. If m is the mass of the particle and V its linear Velocity then its momentum is P = mv

Momentum is denoted by P.

It is a Vector quantity.

If the direction of momentum is same as that of Velocity.

S.I unit of momentum P = mv.

What is Linear momentum?

P = g cm/s.

S.I unit of momentum is kg m/s.

C.G.S unit of momentum is g cm/s.

Case – I

If m = constant then p α v. It means that if two different bodies have same mass then momentum will be greater for the body moving faster.

Case-II

If V = Constant. Then p α m.

It means that if the body have same speed the momentum will be greater for heavy bodies.

In P = mv

If M > m then PM > pm. It means that heavier one has greater momentum

Case – III

If two objects have equal momentum i.e. P = constant then

Example :- Question :-

A body of mass 3kg is moving with a velocity of 2m /s in the east direction. What is the linear momentum of the body? What is its direction?

P = mv.

P = 3×2

P = 6kg m/s. towards east.

Q. How much momentum will a dumb-bell of mass 10kg transfer to the floor if it falls from a height of 80 cm? Take its downward acceleration to be 10m /s2.

U = o, h = d = 80cm, Acceleration = g = 10 m/s2

V2 = u2 + 2as,

V2 = 02 + 2× 10×80100

V2 = o+20×80100

V2=16

V=16

Newton's Second law of Motion

According to Newton 2nd Law of motion the rate of change of momentum of a body is proportional to the external force acting on it and takes place in the direction of force.

According to Newton's 2nd law :-

Force α Change in rate of momentum. Or

F α Δ PΔ+

Or

F αΔ (m v)Δ+

Since the mass of the body remains Constant for small velocities and momentum is measured by the product of mass and velocity , the momentum can change only due to the change in velocity.

F α mΔ vΔ+

We know that rate of change of velocity with respect to time is known as acceleration.

Δ V Δ+ =a

Or, F α ma.

Or, F = Kma

Where K=Constant of proportionality.

If m=1, a=1, then F=1.

Put this value in equation

F = k×1×1

1 = k×1

From equation (i) and (ii)

F = ma

K = 1

Meaning of arrow :-

The direction of acceleration of a body is same as that of the force acting on it.

Q. A body of mass 2kg is pulled by a constant force so that its acceleration is 1 m/s2 towards north. Find the magnitude and direction of the force.

F= ma.

F=2N,towards north

F=2×1

Q. A hockey ball of mass 200g travelling at 10m/s is struck by a hockey stick so as to return it a long its original part with a velocity at 5m/s calculate change of momentum occurred in the motion of the hockey ball by the force applied by the hockey stick.

M= 2001000 kg, u= 10m/s.

V= -5m/s.

Change in momentum= mv-mu.

m (v-a)

=2001000×(-5-10)

=15×-15

= -3 kg m/s

Q. An object of mass 100kg is accelerated uniformly from a velocity of 5m/s to 8m/s in 6 second. Calculate the initial and final momentum of the object, also find the magnitude of the force exerted on the object.

Mass of the object = 100kg,

U = 5m/s, V = 8m/s, T = 6 sec.

Acceleration = (V-Ut)

= (8-56)

= 36

= 0.5m/s2

Force = ma

F = 100 ×0.510

F = 50N

Rate of change of momentum = mv – mu = m(v-u)

Initial momentum = mu

= 100 × 5

= 500m/s

Final momentum = mv.

= 100 × 8

= 800m/s

Q. Two objects each of mass 1.5kg are moving in the same straight line but in opposite direction. The velocity of each object is 2.5 m/s before the collision during which they stick together, what will be the velocity of the combined object after the collision.

m1u1 + m2u2 = m1v1 + m2v2

$1.5 \times 2.5 + 1.5 \times -2.5 = v 1.5 + 1.5$

$1.5 \times 2.5 - 1.5 \times 2.5 = v\ 3.0$

$0 = 3v$

V = 0m/s.

Unit of Force

The force is expressed eighter in absolute or in gravitational units.

Absolute unit of Forces:-

An absolute unit of force which produces in a unit mass for a unit acceleration.

The absolute unit of force is in CGS system and SI system are dyne and Newton. (Expressed by the symbols dyne and N).

Dyne and Newton both the words are well known to us. We all study about that in class 9. But If we have remembered that there would be a relation exist between Dyne and Newton. So before we start discussing about relation. we should have recall both the terms Dyne and Newton in detail. After that we not only established the relation between Newton and Dyne but also derive the relation.

What is Newton?

Newton is the S.I unit of force. Which is denoted by N. Apart from this concept. Newton was a scientist. He discovered gravitation, and also very famous three laws of motion. He also write some novel on optics, calculus etc.

One Newton is defined as: A body of mass 1 kg travelling with the acceleration of 1m/s2. means 1 N = 1kg ✖ 1m/s2.

F = ma

Newton = kg . m/s2.

What is Dyne?

It is the C.G.S unit of force. It is denoted by "Dyne". If we define one dyne then it is a body of one gram of mass travelling with the acceleration of one centimeter per second square. i.e, 1 Dyne = 1g ✖ 1cm/s2.

F = ma

Dyne = 1g . cm/s2

Relation between Dyne and Newton

The mathematical relation between Newton and Dyne is, one newton is equal to the ten to the power five dyne. i.e,

1 Newton = 10^5 Dyne

In other words, the main relation between newton and dyne is both the term has same property. Means both have a unit of Force. But the difference is one have S.I unit and other is C.G.S unit.

S.I unit of force is Newton

C.G.S unit of force is Dyne.

Derivation of relation between Newton and Dyne

Here below are the derivation of relation between Dyne and Newton.

As we know that Force is the product of mass and acceleration. That means in mathematical terms F = ma. we also studied that force is the cross product of mass and acceleration.

F = ma

Force = mass x acceleration

Force = kg x m/s2 --------------- (1)

Now, change it in C.G.S unit. then,

Force = 1000 gram x 100 cm/s2 ------------ (2)

From equ. 1 and 2 we get,

1 kg x 1 m/s2 = 1000 gram x 100 cm/s2

1 Newton (from the definition of one newton) = 1000 x 100 x 1 gram . 1cm/s2

1 Newton = 10^5 x 1 gram . 1 cm/s2

1 Newton = 10^5 x 1 Dyne (from the definition of 1 Dyne)

1 Newton = 10^5 Dyne

Hence, the relation between Dyne and Newton is 1 Newton = 10^5 Dyne.

Gravitational or Practical Unit of Force

A gravitational unit of force is defined as the force with which a body of unit mass is attracted by the earths towards its center.

The gravitational unit of force in CGS system and SI unit are gram Force and kilogram Force (also called gram weight) and Kilogram weight respectively.

Newton's First laws of motion is contained in the second law of motion

According to the Newton first law of motion the position of object does not change if external force is not applied.

So if no external force is acting on the body then,

F = 0 N

Now, According to 2nd law of motion

F = ma

a = Fm

a = 0m

a = 0

= v2 – v1t2-t1 = 0

= v2 – v1 = 0

V2 = v1

It means that if no external force is applied on a moving object then its initial and final velocities are equal. i.e, there is no change in the state of motion or velocity.

Hence, we can say that first law of motion is contained in the second law of motion.

What is Impulse?

Or Change In Momentum :- The Impulse of a force acting on a body is equal to the product of the force and the time for which it acts on a body.

A Force which acts upon a body for a very short time is called an impulsive force.

Impulse as the product of force and the time for which the force acts and its is equal to the total change in momentum.

It is denoted by I.

$I = F \times t$

Impulse is a vector quantity. Its direction is same as that of change in momentum of force.

Impulse = Change in momentum

$F \times t = mv - mu$

$F \times t = m(v-u)$

Application of Impulse

While catching a fast moving cricket ball, the players lower his hands along with the ball.

A person falling from a certain height, receive more several injuries if he falls on a cemental floor while, if he falls on a heap of sand or cotton, he had no injuries.

One more examples to illistrate our confusion on impulse. Lets suppose an athelet after finishing a race, runs for a while and stops. He does not stop in its final potision where race ends. He takes some more distance, due to the momentum of his body called impulse or impulsive force.

Newton's Third law of Motion

According to Newton's third law of motion for every action there is an equal and opposite reaction.

Action and reaction do not cancel each other because they acts on different bodies.

Force always occur in pair.

$N = mg$

Action and reaction acts simultanously out of the pair of forces only force can be called action and the other reaction.

In Other Words

"For every action, there is an equal and opposite reaction."

This law states that when one object applies a force on a second object, the second object applies a force of equal magnitude but in the opposite direction on the first object. Essentially, forces always occur in pairs. If one object exerts a force on another, the second object exerts a force of the same size but in the opposite direction.

Key Points:

Action and Reaction: The force applied by the first object is called the action force, and the force applied by the second object is called the reaction force.

Equal Magnitude: The action and reaction forces have the same size, meaning they are of equal magnitude.

Opposite Directions: These forces act in exactly opposite directions.

Different Objects: Although the action and reaction forces are equal and opposite, they act on different objects, not on the same object. This is important because the forces do not cancel each other out.

Examples of Newton's Third Law:

- Walking:

When you walk, your foot pushes backward on the ground (action), and in response, the ground pushes forward on your foot with an equal force (reaction). This forward push from the ground propels you forward.

- Swimming:

A swimmer pushes the water backward with their hands (action). In response, the water pushes the swimmer forward (reaction), allowing them to move through the water.

- Recoil of a Gun:

When a gun is fired, the bullet is pushed forward out of the barrel (action), and the gun experiences a recoil, pushing backward (reaction).

- Jumping off a Boat:

When you jump off a boat into water, you push the boat backward (action), and the boat pushes you forward (reaction).

- Rocket Launch:

A rocket expels gas downward through its engines (action), and as a result, it is pushed upward with an equal and opposite force (reaction). This is the principle behind rocket propulsion.

Why is this Important?

Balance of Forces: Newton's Third Law helps explain how motion is generated and how objects interact with each other. It underscores the fact that forces are always mutual; one object cannot exert a force without the other object exerting an equal and opposite force back.

Applications in Technology: This law is critical in understanding how machines, vehicles, and even natural systems work. For example, understanding action and reaction forces is crucial for the design of engines, vehicles, and structures that must handle forces efficiently.

Summary:

Newton's Third Law highlights the fundamental symmetry of the universe's interactions: every force has a counterpart that is equal in magnitude but opposite in direction. It governs the interactions between objects and is essential in analyzing various physical phenomena, from simple mechanical processes to complex systems like airplanes and rockets.

Laws of conservation of momentum

According to the laws of conservation of momentum total initial momentum is equal to final momentum.

m1u1 + m2u2 = m1v1 + m2v2

The Law of Conservation of Momentum states that the total momentum of a closed system remains constant if no external forces act on it.

In simpler terms, if no external forces (like friction or external pushes) are involved, the momentum of a system of objects remains the same before and after any interaction or collision between the objects in the system.

Mathematically, the law can be expressed as:

Total Initial Momentum=Total Final Momentum\text{Total Initial Momentum} = \text{Total Final Momentum}

Or:

m1u1+m2u2+⋯+mnun = m_1 v_1 + m_2 v_2 +....... + m_n v_n

Where:

m1,m2,...,mn = Masses of the objects

u1,u2,...,un = Initial velocities of the objects

v1,v2,...,vn = Final velocities of the objects

This equation means that the total momentum before an interaction (like a collision) is equal to the total momentum after the interaction, provided no external force acts on the system.

Key Points of the Law of Conservation of Momentum:

Momentum:

Momentum (p) is the product of an object's mass and its velocity: p=mvp = mv

Momentum is a vector quantity, meaning it has both magnitude and direction.

Closed System:

A closed system refers to a group of objects that do not exchange matter with the outside world and are only subject to internal forces, not external forces.

Collision:

In elastic collisions, both kinetic energy and momentum are conserved.

In inelastic collisions, only momentum is conserved, but some kinetic energy is lost, typically converted into other forms like heat or sound.

External Forces:

If external forces (e.g., friction, external pushes) are negligible or absent, the momentum of the system is conserved. However, if external forces are present, they can change the total momentum of the system.

Examples of the Law of Conservation of Momentum:

Collision of Two Balls:

Consider two billiard balls colliding. Before the collision, each ball has its own momentum. After the collision, the total momentum of both balls combined remains the same (assuming no external forces like friction).

Rocket Propulsion:

A rocket launches by expelling gas backward (action), and the reaction force pushes the rocket forward. In this case, the momentum of the rocket and the expelled gas is conserved. Initially, the system (rocket + gas) has zero momentum, and after the expulsion, both the rocket and the gas have equal and opposite momentum.

Elastic Collision of Two Cars:

Imagine two cars colliding on a frictionless surface. If the collision is perfectly elastic, both momentum and kinetic energy are conserved. The total momentum of the two cars before and after the collision will remain the same.

Walking:

When you walk, your legs push backward on the ground (action), and in response, the ground pushes you forward (reaction). The system of you and the Earth has conserved momentum, with the forces between you and the ground being internal forces.

Applications of the Law of Conservation of Momentum:

Analysis of Collisions:

The law is widely used to analyze collisions in physics, whether elastic or inelastic. It allows us to calculate the final velocities of objects after the collision, given their initial velocities and masses.

Rocket Science and Propulsion:

Rocket propulsion works on the principle of conservation of momentum. When a rocket expels fuel out of its engines (action), it gains forward momentum (reaction). The total momentum of the system (rocket and expelled fuel) remains constant.

Sports:

In sports like billiards or pool, the law of conservation of momentum is crucial to understanding the interactions between the balls after a collision. The direction and speed of the balls after the collision depend on their initial velocities and masses.

Safety in Vehicles:

The law helps design safety features in cars. In the event of a collision, knowing the principles of momentum conservation allows engineers to design crumple zones and airbags that help reduce the impact force on the occupants.

Conclusion:

The Law of Conservation of Momentum is a fundamental principle in physics that holds true in all interactions where external forces are negligible. It applies to various scenarios, from simple collisions in sports to complex systems like rockets and particle interactions. This law is crucial for understanding how objects behave when they interact and is foundational in mechanics.

CHAPTER FOUR

Gravitation

Gravitation Introduction

Gravitation is one of the fundamental forces of nature, responsible for the attraction between objects with mass. It governs the motion of celestial bodies, keeps planets in orbit around stars, and influences the trajectories of objects here on Earth.

Gravitation was first systematically described by Sir Isaac Newton in the 17th century with his Law of Universal Gravitation, which posited that every point mass attracts every other point mass in the universe with a force proportional to the product of their masses and inversely proportional to the square of the distance between them. Newton's work provided the foundation for much of classical mechanics and helped explain the orbits of planets, the motion of objects on Earth, and many other physical phenomena.

However, in the early 20th century, Albert Einstein expanded upon Newton's ideas with his theory of General Relativity. According to General Relativity, gravitation is not a force in the traditional sense, but rather a curvature of spacetime caused by mass and energy. Objects move along curved paths, or geodesics, due to the bending of spacetime by massive objects like planets, stars, and black holes.

Gravitation is a force that operates over long distances, and while it is incredibly weak compared to other fundamental forces (like electromagnetism), it is always attractive and acts over infinite distances. This makes it particularly important in the structure and dynamics of the universe.

Key points in the study of gravitation include:

Gravitational Force: The attraction between masses, described by Newton's Law and influenced by the curvature of spacetime in General Relativity.

Gravitational Fields: The influence that a massive object exerts on its surrounding space.

Gravitational Potential: The potential energy associated with a mass in a gravitational field, determining how it moves under the influence of gravity.

Black Holes: Regions in space where gravity is so intense that not even light can escape.

Overall, gravitation is crucial to understanding the structure and behavior of everything from everyday objects to galaxies, black holes, and the universe as a whole.

What is Gravitational Force?

Gravitation refers to the force of attraction that pulls objects towards the Earth (or any other celestial body). This force is responsible for keeping planets in orbit, causing objects to fall to the ground, and determining the weight of an object.

Gravitational Force: It is the attractive force that exists between any two masses. This force depends on the mass of the objects and the distance between them.

Universal Law of Gravitation

Statement: Every particle of matter in the universe attracts every other particle with a force that is directly proportional to the product of their masses and inversely proportional to the square of the distance between them.

F=G×m1×m2/r2

Where:

F is the gravitational force between the masses.

G is the universal gravitational constant, G=6.674×10−11 N·m2/kg2G = 6.674 10^{-11}

m1m_1 and m2m_2 are the masses of the two objects.

rr is the distance between the centers of the two masses.

Key points:

Gravitational force is always attractive.

It acts on all objects with mass.

It is a long-range force, though weak compared to other forces like electromagnetism.

Acceleration Due to Gravity (g)

Definition: The acceleration produced in an object due to the gravitational force exerted by the Earth (or any other celestial body) is called acceleration due to gravity.

Value of gg: On the surface of the Earth, the value of gg is approximately 9.8 m/s29.8 \, \text{m/s}^2.

Formula for Gravitational Force on Earth:

F=m×gF = m \times g

Where:

FF is the weight of the object (force).

mm is the mass of the object.

gg is the acceleration due to gravity.

Note: g is different on different planets depending on the mass and radius of the planet.

Gravitational Potential Energy

Gravitational potential energy (GPE) is the energy an object possesses due to its position in a gravitational field. It depends on the object's mass, the height at which it is positioned relative to a reference point (usually the Earth's surface), and the strength of the gravitational field acting on it. In simple terms, it is the stored energy that an object has because of its ability to fall under the influence of gravity.

Formula for Gravitational Potential Energy (Near Earth's Surface)

For an object near the Earth's surface, the gravitational potential energy can be calculated using the following equation:

U=mghU = mgh

Where:

U is the gravitational potential energy (in joules, J),

mm is the mass of the object (in kilograms, kg),

gg is the acceleration due to gravity (approximately 9.8 m/s , 29.8 {m/s}^2 on the surface of the Earth),

h is the height of the object above a reference level (usually the ground or Earth's surface, in meters, m).

Conceptual Understanding:

Higher Position = More Potential Energy: An object higher up has more gravitational potential energy because it has a greater distance to fall, and thus more energy to release when it falls.

Work Done in Lifting an Object: If you lift an object to a certain height, you do work against the force of gravity. The amount of work done to lift it becomes the gravitational potential energy that the object has at that height.

Reference Point: Gravitational potential energy is always relative to some reference point. If you choose the ground as the reference point (h=0h = 0), then the potential energy at any height hh is positive. However, you could choose a different reference point, such as the top of a hill, where the potential energy might be negative at lower points.

Gravitational Potential Energy in Space

When an object is far from Earth or another massive body, such as in outer space, the equation for gravitational potential energy becomes more complex because the gravitational force decreases with distance from the source of gravity.

The general formula for gravitational potential energy between two objects, such as a mass mm and a planet of mass MM, separated by a distance rr, is:

U=−GMmrU = - \{GMm}{r}

Where:

- U is the gravitational potential energy (in joules, J),
- G is the gravitational constant (6.67430×10−11 N·m2/ kg26.67430 \times 10^{-11} \, {N} c. t{m}^2/{kg}^2),
- M is the mass of the larger object (in kilograms, kg),
- mm is the mass of the smaller object (in kilograms, kg),
- r is the distance between the centers of mass of the two objects (in meters, m).

Key Points About Gravitational Potential Energy:

Zero Point of GPE: Gravitational potential energy is relative, and its zero point can be chosen based on convenience. For objects near Earth's surface, h=0h = 0 is often taken to be the reference point (ground level). In space, the potential energy becomes negative because the object is moving closer to a massive body (like Earth) and thus becomes more "bound" to it.

Conservation of Energy: Gravitational potential energy is part of the overall energy of a system. As an object falls, its gravitational potential energy is converted into kinetic energy (the energy of motion). The total energy remains conserved, meaning the sum of potential and kinetic energy stays constant, assuming no external forces (like air resistance) are at play.

Escaping Gravity: In the case of space travel, an object must acquire enough energy (i.e., kinetic energy) to overcome the gravitational potential energy of a planet or other body in order to escape its gravitational pull. This is known as "escape velocity."

Examples:

Lifting an Object: If you lift a 10 kg object 5 meters off the ground, its gravitational potential energy increases by:

U=mgh=(10 kg)(9.8 m/s2)(5 m)=490 J

So, the object now has 490 joules of gravitational potential energy.

A Falling Object: If the same object were to fall from that height, the potential energy would convert into kinetic energy as it gains speed. Just before it hits the ground, all of the 490 J of potential energy would have transformed into kinetic energy.

Conclusion:

Gravitational potential energy is a critical concept in both classical and modern physics. It helps explain why objects behave the way they do under gravity, from simple everyday phenomena like dropping a ball to the complex motions of planets and satellites. By understanding how potential energy works, we gain insights into the forces that shape our universe and the principles of energy conservation.

6. Weight of an Object

Definition: Weight is the force exerted on an object due to gravity. It is the product of the mass of the object and the acceleration due to gravity.

Formula:

W=m×gW = m \times g

Where:

WW is the weight of the object (in Newtons).

mm is the mass of the object (in kilograms).

g is the acceleration due to gravity (in m/s2

Note: Weight is a force and is measured in Newtons (N). It can change if the object is taken to a place where gg is different, such as the Moon or another planet.

7. The Gravitational Constant (G)

Definition: It is a proportional constant used in the universal law of gravitation. Its value is the same everywhere in the universe.

Value of GG: G=6.674×10−11 N·m2/kg2G = 6.674

This constant allows us to calculate the gravitational force between two masses.

8. Variation in the Value of g

The acceleration due to gravity gg varies with:

Altitude: As the altitude increases (such as moving away from Earth's surface), the value of gg decreases.

Latitude: The value of gg is slightly less at the equator and greater at the poles due to the Earth's rotation and its oblate shape.

Depth: As we move deeper into the Earth, the value of gg decreases. The gravity decreases because the mass above the object is reducing as we go deeper.

9. Kepler's Laws of Planetary Motion (Brief Overview)

Kepler's Laws of Planetary Motion

Johannes Kepler, a German astronomer in the early 17th century, formulated three laws of planetary motion that describe the orbits of planets around the Sun. These laws revolutionized our understanding of the solar system and laid the groundwork for Isaac Newton's later work on gravitation. Kepler's laws were derived from the meticulous observations of the planets made by Tycho Brahe, his mentor, and they describe the motion of planets with a high degree of precision.

1. Kepler's First Law – The Law of Ellipses

Statement: The orbit of every planet is an ellipse with the Sun at one of the two foci.

An ellipse is a stretched-out circle, characterized by two focal points. In this law, one focus of the ellipse is occupied by the Sun, while the other focus is empty. This means that the planets do not move in perfect circular orbits, but rather in elliptical paths around the Sun.

Key Concepts:

Perihelion: The closest point in a planet's orbit to the Sun.

Aphelion: The farthest point in a planet's orbit from the Sun.

Eccentricity: A measure of how "elongated" or "stretched" the ellipse is. If eccentricity is 0, the orbit is a perfect circle. If it is close to 1, the orbit is very elongated.

Significance: Prior to Kepler, many astronomers believed that planetary orbits were circular. Kepler's first law showed that they are elliptical, which was a crucial correction to the classical view.

2. Kepler's Second Law – The Law of Equal Areas

Statement: A line segment joining a planet and the Sun sweeps out equal areas during equal intervals of time.

This law implies that a planet moves faster when it is closer to the Sun and slower when it is farther away. The area swept by the line connecting the planet and the Sun remains constant over equal time intervals.

Key Concepts:

When the planet is near perihelion (closest to the Sun), it moves faster along its orbit.

When the planet is near aphelion (farthest from the Sun), it moves slower.

Significance: This law is a direct consequence of the conservation of angular momentum. As a planet moves in its elliptical orbit, it must adjust its speed in such a way that the area swept out by the line between it and the Sun remains the same, regardless of where the planet is in its orbit.

3. Kepler's Third Law – The Harmonic Law

Statement: The square of the orbital period of a planet is directly proportional to the cube of the semi-major axis of its orbit.

Mathematically, this law is expressed as:

T2∝a3T^2 \propto a^3

Where:

T is the orbital period (the time it takes for a planet to complete one orbit around the Sun).

aa is the semi-major axis of the planet's orbit, which is the average distance between the planet and the Sun.

For example, the Earth takes approximately 1 year to orbit the Sun, and its average distance from the Sun is about 1 AU (astronomical unit). For Jupiter, which is farther from the Sun, its orbital period is much longer.

Significance: Kepler's third law demonstrated that there is a precise mathematical relationship between the distance of a planet from the Sun and the time it takes to complete an orbit. This was a critical observation that Newton later incorporated into his law of gravitation.

Summary of Kepler's Laws

First Law (Elliptical Orbits): Planets orbit the Sun in elliptical paths, with the Sun at one focus of the ellipse.

Second Law (Equal Areas): A planet sweeps out equal areas in equal times, meaning it moves faster when closer to the Sun and slower when farther away.

Third Law (Harmonic Law): The square of the orbital period is proportional to the cube of the semi-major axis of the orbit. This means that planets farther from the Sun take longer to orbit.

Applications of Kepler's Laws

Predicting Planetary Positions: Kepler's laws allow astronomers to calculate the positions of planets at any given time, which is essential for space missions and satellite navigation.

Understanding Orbital Mechanics: The laws also apply to the motion of artificial satellites and moons, not just planets, as they are governed by the same principles.

Kepler's Laws in Modern Physics: Kepler's work laid the foundation for Newton's theory of gravitation. Newton used Kepler's laws to derive his universal law of gravitation, which describes the gravitational force between two objects.

Kepler's Legacy

Kepler's laws were groundbreaking because they introduced a precise, empirical description of planetary motion, rejecting the ancient notion of circular orbits. His work transformed our understanding of the cosmos, helping to establish the heliocentric model of the solar system, which was later refined by Newton and others. Kepler's laws remain fundamental to the study of orbital mechanics in astronomy and physics today.

10. Satellite Motion

Artificial Satellites: These are human-made objects that orbit the Earth or other celestial bodies.

Gravitational Force on Satellites: A satellite remains in orbit due to the balance between the gravitational force pulling it toward the Earth and its inertia trying to move it in a straight line. This balance allows it to stay in a stable orbit.

Orbital Speed and Period: The speed required for a satellite to stay in orbit depends on the mass of the planet and the distance from the center of the planet. The time taken for one complete orbit is called the orbital period.

11. Escape Velocity

Escape velocity is the minimum speed that an object must have in order to escape the gravitational influence of a celestial body, such as Earth, without further propulsion. This means that at this speed, an object will not fall back to the planet or other body but will break free and move away from it indefinitely (ignoring other forces like air resistance).

Key Concepts of Escape Velocity:

No Further Propulsion Needed: Once an object reaches escape velocity, it does not need any more thrust or propulsion. The object will continue to move away from the celestial body, its kinetic energy gradually converting to gravitational potential energy, until it reaches a point where it no longer feels the gravitational pull.

Energy Considerations: The escape velocity is based on the concept of energy conservation. For an object to escape the gravitational pull of a planet, its kinetic energy must be enough to overcome its gravitational potential energy.

Gravitational Potential Energy: This is the energy associated with an object's position in a gravitational field. The higher the object is, the greater its potential energy. The object needs to gain enough kinetic energy to counteract this pull.

Escape Velocity and Different Planets

Earth: As shown above, the escape velocity from the surface of Earth is about 11.2 km/s.

Moon: The escape velocity from the Moon, which has much lower mass and radius than Earth, is about 2.4 km/s.

Mars: For Mars, the escape velocity is approximately 5.0 km/s.

Jupiter: Due to its large mass and size, Jupiter's escape velocity is much higher, about 60 km/s.

The escape velocity depends both on the mass and the radius of the celestial body. A larger mass (higher gravitational pull) and a smaller radius (closer proximity to the center of the body) will result in a higher escape velocity.

Escape Velocity and Energy Considerations

To understand why escape velocity works the way it does, it's useful to consider energy:

Gravitational Potential Energy: The gravitational potential energy of an object at a distance rr from the center of a body of mass MM is given by:

U=−GMmrU

Where mm is the mass of the object and UU is negative because the object is bound by gravity.

Kinetic Energy: The kinetic energy (KK) of an object is: K=12mv2

For the object to escape the gravitational field, the total mechanical energy (the sum of kinetic and potential energy) must be zero or positive. That is:

Kinetic Energy=Gravitational Potential Energy\text{Kinetic Energy} = \text{Gravitational Potential Energy}

Thus, at the point where an object just escapes the planet's gravitational influence, the kinetic energy is exactly equal to the negative of the gravitational potential energy. This gives rise to the equation for escape velocity.

Practical Considerations

Air Resistance: The formula for escape velocity assumes there is no atmospheric drag, which would be the case in a vacuum. In reality, objects launched from the Earth's surface must overcome air resistance, which requires additional velocity or propulsion.

Rockets: In practice, rockets don't reach escape velocity in a single step. They gradually increase their velocity over time as they ascend and burn fuel. The concept of escape velocity, however, gives a theoretical minimum speed required to escape the gravitational pull of a planet.

Escape Beyond the Solar System: If an object is launched at a speed greater than the escape velocity from the Sun's gravitational field (about 42 km/s at Earth's distance), it could escape the solar system entirely, moving into interstellar space.

Summary of Key Points:

Escape velocity is the minimum speed an object needs to escape the gravitational pull of a celestial body.

It depends on the mass of the celestial body and the distance from its center.

For Earth, the escape velocity is approximately 11.2 km/s at the surface.

The escape velocity is independent of the mass of the object trying to escape — only the mass of the body being escaped from and the distance from its center matter.

In practice, escape velocity is a theoretical concept and does not mean an object must achieve that speed instantaneously. Rockets gradually increase speed to achieve escape velocity.

Understanding escape velocity is essential for space exploration, satellite launches, and understanding how objects move in the gravitational fields of planets, moons, and stars.

CHAPTER FIVE

Work Energy And Power

Work, Energy, and Power: A Comprehensive Guide

Introduction

Work, energy, and power are fundamental concepts in physics that explain how objects move and interact with forces. These three concepts form the backbone of classical mechanics and have wide applications in various fields like engineering, mechanics, and daily life. Let's dive into each of them in detail.

1. Work

Definition:

In physics, work is defined as the transfer of energy when a force is applied to an object, causing it to move in the direction of the force. Work is done when a force moves an object over a distance.

Formula:

The mathematical expression for work is:

Work(W)=Force(F)×Displacement(d)×cos θ

Where:

W is the work done (in joules, J),

F is the applied force (in newtons, N),

d is the displacement of the object (in meters, m),

θ is the angle between the direction of the applied force and the displacement.

Conditions for Work:

The object must move.

The force must cause displacement in the direction of the force.

The force can be constant or variable.

Significance of the Cosine Term:

When the force is applied in the direction of the displacement ($\theta=0^\circ$), the work done is maximum, as $\cos 0^\circ =1$

If the force is perpendicular to the displacement ($\theta=90^\circ$), no work is done, as $\cos 90^\circ =0$

2. Energy

Definition:

Energy is the capacity to do work. It is a scalar quantity and can exist in various forms such as kinetic energy, potential energy, thermal energy, etc. Energy cannot be created or destroyed but can only be converted from one form to another.

Units of Energy:

The SI unit of energy is the Joule (J), which is also the unit of work. One joule of energy is used when a force of one newton moves an object by one meter in the direction of the force.

Types of Energy:

Kinetic Energy (KE):

Kinetic energy is the energy possessed by an object due to its motion. It is given by the formula:

KE=12mv2

Where:

m is the mass of the object (in kg),

v is the velocity of the object (in m/s).

Key Points:

The kinetic energy of an object increases with its speed and mass.

Kinetic energy is always positive, as both mass and velocity are squared.

Potential Energy (PE):

Potential energy is the energy stored in an object due to its position relative to a force, such as gravity. The most common form of potential energy is gravitational potential energy, given by the formula:

PE=mgh

Where:

m is the mass of the object (in kg),

g is the acceleration due to gravity (9.8 m/s^2 on Earth), h is the height of the object above a reference point (in meters).

Key Points:

The higher an object is above the ground, the more gravitational potential energy it has.

When an object falls, its potential energy is converted into kinetic energy.

Other Forms of Energy:

Elastic Potential Energy (e.g., in a stretched spring),

Chemical Energy (e.g., in food, fuel),

Thermal Energy (due to the movement of particles in matter),

Electromagnetic Energy (in the form of light, X-rays, etc.).

Law of Conservation of Energy:

Energy can neither be created nor destroyed; it only changes from one form to another. This is known as the law of conservation of energy, which states that the total energy in an isolated system remains constant over time.

3. Power

Definition:

Power is the rate at which work is done or energy is transferred. It measures how quickly work can be done or energy can be converted.

Formula:

The formula for power is:

$P=W/t$

Where:
P is the power (in watts, W),
W is the work done or energy transferred (in joules, J),
t is the time taken (in seconds, s).

Units of Power:

The SI unit of power is the watt (W). One watt is equal to one joule per second (J/s).

1 W = 1 J/s

Other Units:

Horsepower (hp): A unit used to measure power, especially in engines. 1 horsepower = 746 watts.

Power in Relation to Energy:

If the same amount of work is done in a shorter time, the power required is greater.

If a task is performed over a longer time, the power required is less.

4. Relationship Between Work, Energy, and Power

Work and Energy: Work is the process of transferring energy. When work is done on an object, energy is transferred to or from the object. Energy can be stored (as potential energy) or in motion (as kinetic energy).

Power and Work: Power is the rate at which work is done or energy is transferred. For a given amount of work, if the time taken is reduced, the power required increases.

Formula for Power (in terms of force and velocity):

If a constant force is applied to an object moving with constant velocity, the power can be expressed as:

$P = F \times v$

Where:
F is the force applied (in newtons),
v is the velocity of the object (in meters per second).

5. Applications of Work, Energy, and Power

In Engines:

Power is the rate at which an engine can do work. The more power an engine produces, the faster it can perform work (e.g., accelerating a car).

In Daily Life:

Lifting objects, running machines, and even walking involves work, energy, and power. Power is required to complete these tasks at varying speeds.

In Renewable Energy:

Wind turbines convert kinetic energy from the wind into electrical energy, and power generation depends on the rate at which energy is converted.

In Sports:

Athletes generate power when they perform tasks like sprinting or lifting weights. The ability to do work quickly is crucial in many sports.

6. Summary

Work is the transfer of energy through force and movement.

Energy is the ability to do work and exists in various forms.

Power is the rate at which work is done or energy is transferred.

The law of conservation of energy governs the behavior of energy in an isolated system.

These concepts are essential for understanding the mechanics of everyday objects and systems in motion, from simple machines to complex engines and renewable energy systems.

CHAPTER SIX

Sound And Its Law

What is sound?

- sound is a form of energy.
- All vibrating body produced sound.
- sound is that form of energy which makes us here.
- Sound is a form of energy created by the vibration of particles in a medium.
- It is a mechanical wave that requires a medium (solid, liquid, or gas) to travel.
- Sound travels in the form of longitudinal waves, where particles oscillate back and forth in the direction of wave propagation.
- Frequency determines the pitch of the sound (measured in Hertz, Hz).
- Amplitude determines the loudness of the sound (measured in decibels, dB).
- Sound cannot travel through a vacuum because there are no particles to vibrate.
- The speed of sound varies depending on the medium, being faster in solids and slower in gases.

- Humans typically hear sounds with frequencies between 20 Hz and 20,000 Hz.
- Sound can be reflected (echoes), absorbed, or refracted depending on the environment.
- It plays a key role in communication, navigation, and various technologies (e.g., sonar, ultrasound).

Characteristic of sound.

Sound needs a material medium to travels.

Medium:- The substance through which sound travels is called a medium.

Note:- Hence we can say sound can travels through a medium solid, liquid and gasses, but it cannot travels through vaccum.

Sound can travels through solid

If a child speaks into one tin he can be here by another child who puts his ear to the other tin. It means that sound can travels through solid.

Sound can travels through liquid

If we fill a balloon with water and hold it near our ear then hit by a finger in lower side of the balloon with some force then we observe that some is hearing, so we conclude by this experiment when we git balloon then water molecules vibrate up and down rapidly and we here sound.

it means that sound can travels through water.

Yes, sound can travel through water. In fact, sound travels faster in water than in air due to the higher density and elasticity of water compared to air.

Water molecules are closer together than air molecules, which allows sound waves to transfer energy more efficiently. The speed of sound in water is approximately

1,480 meters per second (m/s), which is significantly faster than the speed of sound in air (about 343 m/s at room temperature).

This is why whales and dolphins, for example, use sound to communicate over long distances underwater, and why sonar systems can detect objects and measure distances underwater.

Sound can travels through gasses.

When our parents talk to each other then we here sound because of disturbance of the particles of the air. we know that air is a gas so, sound can travels through gas.

it is the same reason for telephone bell when it ring.

Sound can't travels through vaccum

A material medium (like air) is necessary for propagation of sound.

Characteristic of Sound wave in more Details.

Here are the key characteristics of sound:

Pitch:

- Pitch refers to the perceived frequency of a sound.
- High-pitched sounds have a high frequency (e.g., a whistle), and low-pitched sounds have a low frequency (e.g., a drum).
- It is measured in Hertz (Hz), which represents the number of vibrations or cycles per second.

Loudness:

- Loudness is the perceived intensity or volume of a sound.

- It depends on the amplitude of the sound wave — higher amplitude = louder sound.
- Loudness is measured in decibels (dB).

Timbre (Quality or Color of Sound):

- Timbre refers to the distinctive quality or tone of a sound that allows us to differentiate between different sound sources, even if they have the same pitch and loudness.
- It is what makes a guitar sound different from a piano, even if they play the same note.

Speed:

- The speed of sound is the rate at which sound waves travel through a medium.
- It varies depending on the medium: faster in solids, slower in liquids, and slowest in gases.
- In air, the speed of sound is about 343 meters per second (m/s) at room temperature.

Wavelength:

- Wavelength is the distance between two consecutive compressions or rarefactions in a sound wave.
- It is inversely related to frequency: higher frequency = shorter wavelength.

Reflection:

- When sound waves hit a surface, they bounce back. This is called echo or reverberation.

- Reflection is used in technologies like sonar and ultrasound imaging.

Refraction:

- Refraction occurs when sound waves change direction due to a change in the medium's properties (e.g., temperature or pressure).
- This can cause sound to bend, altering how it's heard at different distances.

Absorption:

- Sound can be absorbed by materials, reducing its intensity.
- Soft materials, such as carpets or curtains, are good at absorbing sound, while hard surfaces like concrete reflect sound.

Diffraction:

- Diffraction refers to the bending of sound waves around obstacles or through openings.
- Sound waves can bend around corners or pass through gaps, which is why we can hear sounds even when we can't see their source.

Resonance:

- Resonance occurs when an object vibrates at its natural frequency in response to an external sound wave.
- This is the principle behind musical instruments and certain acoustic phenomena (e.g., a glass breaking when

a high-pitched sound is played).

- Directionality:
- Sound waves propagate in all directions, but the direction of sound can be influenced by the shape of the environment or the presence of obstacles.
- The directionality of sound is crucial in technologies like microphones and speakers.

These characteristics define the behavior and perception of sound in various environments and applications.

The case of moon and the outer space this happens as follows:-

In outer space there is no air present so we know that for propagation of sound a material medium must be able to carry sound waves from one place to another place but there is no material medium is present so sound cannot travels through vaccum. also sound cannot be hered in outer space or even in any place where air is not present then sound cannot travels on there. for propagation of sound there is very - very necessary a material medium like air.

We cannot be talked on the moon like on the earth so space man can talk by radio wave. radio wave can travels through vaccum or in empty space because it an electromagnetic wave. we discuss about electromagnetic waves in latter topic.

Sound travels in the form of waves

sound travels in the form of wave or even light also travels in the form of waves. we all know that sound is a form of energy so wave carry energy. wave is a vibrating disturbance in the air which carry energy from one place to another place.

Sound is a disturbance in the the medium and it is also a form of energy so sound wave carry energy from one point to another point.

If we through a stone into a pond then we saw a concentric circle in the pond produced that is called the wave of sound namely transverse wave.

when a water waves passes over the surface of the water in a pond, there is no actual movement of water from the center to the side of the pond only the water molecules vibrates up and down about their fixed positions due to this reason water molecules appears to be moving to us.

A periodic disturbance produce in a material medium due to the vibrating motion of the particles of medium is called wave.

Wave motion

It is the movement of disturbance produce to in one part of a medium to another involving the transfer of energy but not the transfer of matter, is called wave motion.

example:- Formation of ripples on the water surface. and propagation of sound wave through air or any other material medium.

Characteristic of wave motion

In wave motion the particles of the medium vibrate about their mean position. the particls of the medium do not move from one place to another place.

A wave motion travels by the same speed in all direction from the sound producing object in any medium.

In wave motion medium do not moves but the disturbance travels through the medium.

During a wave motion energy is transfer from one point of the medium to the another there is no transfer of matter through the medium.

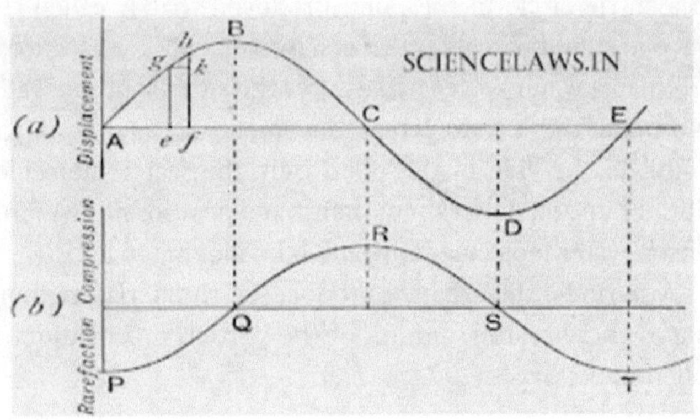

Mechanical wave and Non mechanical wave

Mechanical wave:-

- The wave which need a material medium for their propagation are called mechanical wave.
- The medium may be solid, liquid or gas.
- Mechanical wave propagate through a medium due to the elastic properties of the medium due to this reason mechanical wave are also called elastic wave.
- Mechanical waves cannot travels through vaccum.
- Mechanical waves may be longitudinal, transverse wave.

- Speed of mechanical waves are low and depends upon the source and the medium through which they travels.
- Mechanical waves are due to the vibrations of the particles of the medium.
- Example of mechanical waves are sound waves and water waves.

Non mechanical wave:-

- The wave which do not need any material medium for their propagation of the sound is called non mechanical wave.
- Non mechanical wave can also travels through a material medium as well as vaccum.
- Electromagnetic waves are also called non mechanical waves.
- Light waves are non mechanical waves.
- Non mechanical wave can travels through vaccum.

Electromagnetic wave

- The wave which are associated with oscillating electrical and magnetic field and which do not need any material medium for the propagation of sound are called electromagnetic wave.
- electromagnetic wave can even travels through vaccum. ex. light waves, redio waves, television wave and x ray are electromagnetic waves.
- Electromagnetic waves are transverse wave.

- Electromagnetic waves travels with a speed of 3 x 10^8 m/s.
- The speed of an electromagnetic waves in any material medium is less then that in vaccum.
- Sound waves travels with low speed about 344 m/s at 20° C in air.
- Light wave and radio wave travels with velocity of light.

Longitudinal wave and Transverse wave

<u>Longitudinal wave:-</u>

In this wave particles of the medium vibrate to and fro about their mean position in the direction of propagation of the wave is called a longitudinal wave.

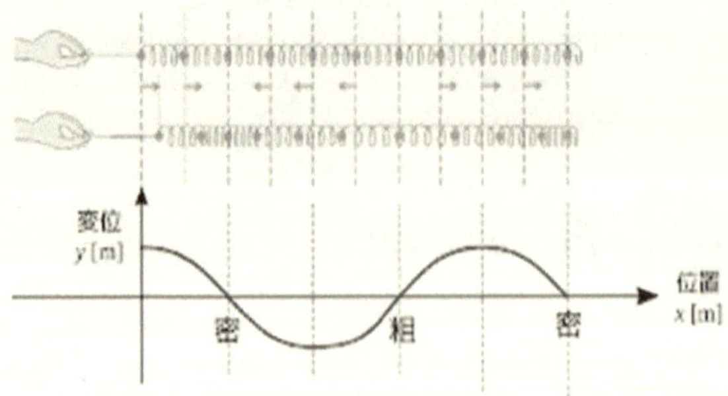

The wave which travels along a spring when it is pushed and pulled at one end are called longitudinal wave.

Longitudinal wave can be produced in any medium (like solid, liquid or gas) . ex:- when a sound wave passes through air the particles of air vibrate back and forth parallel to the direction of sound wave.

When the vibrating particles come closer to one another then their is a movementry reduction in volume and a compression is formed, on the other hand when the vibrating particles apart from one another then they normally their is a movementry increases in volume and a rarefaction is formed.

Experiment to show that how compression and rarefaction is formed in air.

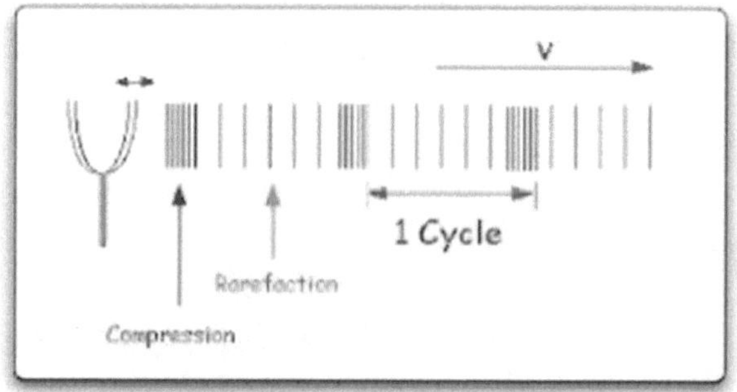

Compression

It is the part of a longitudinal wave in which the particles of the medium are closer to one another.

Compression is a key concept in the behavior of sound waves. Here's an explanation in bullet points:

- Definition:

Compression refers to the region of high pressure in a longitudinal sound wave, where the particles of the medium (such as air or water) are closer together due to the vibration of the source.

- How It Works:

In a sound wave, the particles of the medium vibrate back and forth, creating alternating regions of compression (where particles are close together) and rarefaction (where particles are spread apart).

When the vibrating object (like a speaker or a tuning fork) moves outward, it pushes particles together, creating compression.

- Role in Sound:

Compression is responsible for the transfer of energy through the medium in a sound wave.

The alternating compressions and rarefactions travel through the medium, carrying the sound from the source to the listener.

- Characteristics of Compression:

Compression represents the maximum displacement of particles towards each other in the wave cycle.

It occurs at the same time as rarefaction, forming a complete sound wave.

The density and pressure of the medium are highest in the compression regions.

- Example:

When a drumstick strikes a drum, the air particles in front of the drumhead are compressed, producing a sound wave that travels away from the drum.

In summary, compression is a critical part of sound propagation, creating areas of higher pressure in the medium that help carry the sound energy.

Rarefaction

It is the part of a longitudinal wave in which the particles of the medium are further apart from the normal is called rarefaction.

Rarefaction is the opposite of compression and is another fundamental concept in the behavior of sound waves. Here's an explanation in bullet points.

- Definition:

Rarefaction refers to the region of low pressure in a longitudinal sound wave, where the particles of the medium (such as air, water, or solids) are spread apart due to the vibration of the sound source.

- How It Works:

In a sound wave, as the vibrating object (like a speaker diaphragm or tuning fork) moves backward, it pulls particles apart, creating rarefaction.

Rarefaction occurs immediately after the compression phase in the wave cycle.

- Role in Sound:

Like compression, rarefaction plays an important role in the transfer of energy through the medium.

The alternating pattern of compression and rarefaction propagates through the medium, allowing sound to travel from the source to the listener.

- Characteristics of Rarefaction:

Rarefaction is the region where the density and pressure of the medium are the lowest in the sound wave cycle.

It represents the maximum displacement of particles away from each other in the wave cycle.

The particles in the rarefaction region are further apart than the equilibrium position.

- Example:

When a guitar string vibrates, it creates areas of compression (where air molecules are tightly packed) and rarefaction (where air molecules are more spread out). This alternating pattern of compressions and rarefactions forms a sound wave.

- Summary

Rarefaction is a critical part of how sound waves propagate, creating areas of low pressure where particles in the medium are pulled apart. It works in conjunction with compression to allow sound to travel through the air or other mediums.

Transverse wave

A wave in which the particles of the medium vibrate up and down at right angle to the direction in which the wave is moving is called a transverse wave.

- **Transverse wave can be produced only in solid and liquid but not in gas.**

Example:- when a stone is droped in a pond of water, transverse water waves are produced on the surface of water. even the light wave and radio waves are transverse wave because this wave cannot travels through air we know that transverse wave also cannot consist of medium gases.

- **A transverse wave travels horizontally in a medium, the particles of the medium vibrate up and down in the vertical direction.**

The wave propagates in the form of crest and trough.

These waves can travels through solid and on the surface of liquid only, as the propagation of these waves causes change in the shape of the medium.

As there is no vibration of volume, there is no vibration in the density of the medium while the wave propagates through it.

There is no created in pressure in the medium while the wave propagate.

Transverse wave described Graphically

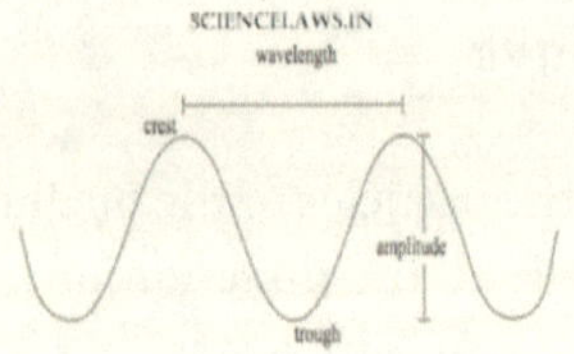

Crest

The point of maximum position displacement on a transverse wave is called a crest.

The term crest is used to describe a specific point in a wave (whether sound, light, or water waves). Here's a breakdown of the concept of a crest in the context of sound waves and general wave theory:

- Definition:

The crest is the highest point or maximum displacement of a wave above the equilibrium or resting position.

It represents the peak of a wave in the cycle, where the particles of the medium (in a transverse wave) are at their greatest distance from their normal, undisturbed position.

- Context in Sound Waves (Longitudinal Waves):

In sound waves (which are longitudinal), the concept of a "crest" is less visually obvious since the sound wave is a compression and rarefaction pattern.

However, in terms of pressure, the crest corresponds to the compression part of the sound wave where the pressure is highest.

Note: In longitudinal waves like sound, we typically refer to compressions and rarefactions, but the crest can metaphorically represent the maximum compression in the wave.

- Context in Transverse Waves:

In transverse waves (like light or water waves), the crest is the highest point in the wave's oscillation above the baseline or equilibrium position.

For example, in a water wave, the crest is the top of the wave that we see as it moves.

- Key Characteristics:

The crest represents the maximum upward displacement (in a transverse wave).

It is the point of maximum energy in many wave phenomena.

The opposite of the crest is the trough, which represents the lowest point of the wave.

- In Sound Waves (Pressure Waves):

Although sound is a longitudinal wave, the analogous concept to the crest (in terms of pressure) is the compression.

The trough in sound waves corresponds to the rarefaction, the area of lower pressure.

- Summary:

In a wave, the crest is the highest point of the wave, where the particles in the medium are displaced the most in the positive direction (or maximum compression in a longitudinal wave). In sound, this corresponds to areas of high pressure (compression) in the sound wave. In other types of waves like light or water, it's simply the highest point above the equilibrium position.

Trough

The trough is the opposite of the crest in a wave. Here's an explanation of the trough in the context of wave theory, particularly with regard to sound waves and general wave behavior:

- Definition:

The trough is the lowest point or maximum displacement of a wave below the equilibrium or resting position.

It represents the bottom of the wave in the wave cycle, where the particles of the medium are at their greatest distance from their normal, undisturbed position.

- Context in Sound Waves (Longitudinal Waves):

In sound waves (which are longitudinal), the trough corresponds to the rarefaction part of the wave, where the pressure is lowest and the particles of the medium are spread furthest apart.

While sound waves don't have visual "peaks" like transverse waves, the rarefaction part is where the particles of the medium are at their maximum displacement away from the resting position, analogous to the trough in a transverse wave.

- Context in Transverse Waves:

In transverse waves (like water waves or light waves), the trough is the lowest point in the oscillation of the wave, occurring below the equilibrium line.

In a water wave, for example, the trough is the bottom part of the wave, where the water level is at its lowest.

- Key Characteristics:

The trough represents the maximum downward displacement in a transverse wave.

In sound waves, it corresponds to areas of low pressure (rarefaction), where the air molecules are spread out.

The opposite of the trough is the crest, which is the highest point of the wave, corresponding to areas of high pressure (compression) in sound waves.

- In Sound Waves (Pressure Waves):

In a longitudinal wave (such as sound), the trough is typically associated with rarefaction, where the air pressure is at its lowest point and the molecules are more spaced out.

Crests and troughs are conceptualized in sound waves as the regions of compression (high pressure) and rarefaction (low pressure), respectively.

- Summary:

The trough is the lowest point in a wave, where the particles of the medium are displaced the most in the negative direction (or maximum rarefaction in a longitudinal wave). In sound, this corresponds to areas of low pressure in the wave. In transverse waves, the trough is simply the lowest part of the oscillation, opposite the crest.

The point of maximum negative depth displacement on a transverse wave is called trough.

characteristics of sound waves

characteristic of a sound wave:- A sound wave can be described by five characteristic these are

1. Wavelength
2. Amplitude
3. Time period
4. Frequency
5. Velocity

Wavelength

- The distance between the two nearest crest of a wave is called its wavelength.

- The minimum distance in which a sound wave repeats itself is called its wavelength.
- In other words it is the length of one complete wave.
- The distance between neighboring crest and trough is equal to half of the wavelength.
- Wavelength is denoted by lambda (λ).
- S.I unit of wavelength is 'm' .

Amplitude

- The height of the crest or the depth of the trough of a wave is called amplitude.
- It is denoted by 'A'.
- Its S.I unit is 'm' .
- The amplitude of a wave is a measure of its energy hence the greater of the amplitude of a wave the greater is the energy.

Frequency

- The number of wave produced per second is called frequency.
- Frequency is denoted by ? or read as (nu) or f.
- The unit of frequency is Hz.
- example:- If 30 waves cycle are produced in one second then the frequency of the periodic wave is 30 Hz or 30 cycle/s.

- Note:- Frequency of a wave does not depend upon the nature of the medium through which it is travels hence the frequency of the wave remains the same as like solid, liquid and gas.

Time period

- The time required to produce on complete wave is called the time period of the wave.
- The S.I unit of time period is second 's' .
- It is denoted by letter 'T'.

Wave velocity

- The distance traveled by wave in one second is called wave velocity.
- It is denoted by letter 'V'.
- The S.I unit of wave velocity is m/s.
- The velocity of the wave depends upon the material medium through which they travels.
- speed of sound in air 343 m/s at 20 degree C.
- Speed of sound depend on medium as I say in the previous line.

Relation between Time period and its frequency

We know that time required to complete one wave is called time period.

Number of wave produce in 'T' sec. = 1

Number of wave produce in 1 sec. = 1/T

but,

we know that No. of wave produce in one second is called frequency,

∴ Frequency = 1/ time period

F = 1/ T

Relation between wave velocity, Frequency and wavelength for a periodic wave.

velocity of wave = wavelength x Frequency

The relationship between wave velocity (v), frequency (f), and wavelength (λ) for a periodic wave is described by the fundamental wave equation:

v=f·λv

Where:

v = Wave velocity (also called wave speed) — the speed at which the wave propagates through the medium (measured in meters per second, m/s).

f = Frequency — the number of oscillations or cycles of the wave that occur per unit of time (measured in hertz, Hz).

λ (lambda) = Wavelength — the distance between two consecutive points that are in phase, such as from one crest to the next, or one compression to the next (measured in meters, m).

Key Points:

- Wave Velocity (v):

Wave velocity is how fast the wave travels through a medium. It depends on the properties of the medium (e.g., its density and elasticity) and is independent of frequency and wavelength for a given medium.

- Frequency (f):

Frequency is the number of wave cycles that pass a point per second. The frequency is determined by the source of the wave (e.g., the vibrating object producing sound or light).

- Wavelength (λ):

Wavelength is the spatial distance between two consecutive points in phase (e.g., from one crest to the next crest or from one compression to the next compression).

- Relationship Explanation:

The wave velocity (v) is equal to the product of frequency (f) and wavelength (λ).

If the frequency of a wave increases, its wavelength must decrease for the wave velocity to remain constant. Conversely, if the frequency decreases, the wavelength increases.

- This is why:

High-frequency waves (like sound in air or light) generally have shorter wavelengths.

Low-frequency waves (like sound waves in the ocean or radio waves) tend to have longer wavelengths.

- Example:

If the speed of sound in air is approximately 343 m/s (at 20°C), and the frequency of a sound wave is 500 Hz, the wavelength (λ) can be calculated as:

$v=f\cdot\lambda$

So, the wavelength of the sound wave is 0.686 meters.

- Summary of the Wave Equation:

Wave Velocity (v) = Frequency (f) × Wavelength (λ)

As frequency increases, wavelength decreases (if wave velocity is constant).

As frequency decreases, wavelength increases (if wave velocity is constant).

This equation is fundamental for understanding the behavior of all types of waves, including sound waves, light waves, and electromagnetic waves.

Sonic Boom

When a body moves with a velocity which is greater than the speed of sound in air then it is said to be travelling at supersonic speed. (such as jet fighter plane or bullet gun), and when they produce a sharp loud sound called a sonic boom.

A sonic boom is a shockwave that is produced when an object travels through the air at a speed faster than the speed of sound. Here's a detailed breakdown of what a sonic boom is, how it occurs, and its effects:

- Definition:

A sonic boom is the loud sound caused by the shockwave created when an object (such as an aircraft) exceeds the speed of sound in the medium it is traveling through (usually air).

How it Occurs:

- Speed of Sound:

The speed of sound in air at sea level and at 20°C (68°F) is approximately 343 meters per second (m/s) or 1,235 kilometers per hour (km/h).

When an object moves faster than this speed, it is said to be traveling at supersonic speeds.

- Shockwave Formation:

As the object moves through the air at supersonic speeds, it compresses the air in front of it.

These compressed air molecules create a pressure wave that propagates outward and funnels into a shockwave.

The shockwave has a conical shape, spreading out from the point where the object is moving, and it travels along with the object.

- Breaking the Sound Barrier:

When the object reaches the speed of sound (Mach 1), it creates a buildup of pressure in front of it.

Once the object exceeds Mach 1, it "breaks" the sound barrier, and the shockwave forms.

This shockwave produces a sudden and very loud sound — the sonic boom — that can be heard over a large area.

- The Sonic Boom Sound:

The sonic boom is not a single "bang" but rather a continuous sound that occurs as the shockwave passes over the observer.

The intensity of the sound depends on the speed of the object, its size, and the altitude at which it is flying.

Key Characteristics of a Sonic Boom:

Loudness: The sound of a sonic boom can be extremely loud, reaching up to 180 decibels (dB). For comparison, jet engines produce about 140 dB, and a typical rock concert might reach 120 dB.

Duration: A sonic boom lasts for a very short time, typically just a few seconds, but it can be heard over a large area.

Shape of the Boom: The boom is not just a sharp "bang" but a wavefront that is heard as the shockwave reaches an observer. It can be heard as a double bang or a continuous crack depending on the observer's position relative to the object's path.

Effects of a Sonic Boom:

Damage:

The intense pressure created by the shockwave can cause damage to buildings, windows, and structures. It can shatter glass and cause minor structural damage.

Increased noise pollution: Repeated sonic booms from aircraft can lead to disturbances in residential areas and contribute to noise pollution.

Distance:

Sonic booms can be heard miles away from the object creating them. The distance from the object that a sonic boom can be heard depends on its speed, altitude, and the atmospheric conditions.

For example, an aircraft flying at 30,000 feet (9,144 meters) can produce a sonic boom that is heard on the ground many miles away.

Aircraft Design:

Modern supersonic aircraft, like the Concorde (which has since been retired), were designed with special aerodynamic features to minimize the effects of sonic booms, such as flying at higher altitudes and maintaining a more controlled supersonic speed.

There is ongoing research into developing quiet supersonic technology (sometimes called "low-boom" technology) to reduce the environmental impact of sonic booms, especially over populated areas.

Sonic Boom and Mach Numbers:

The term Mach number represents the ratio of the speed of an object to the speed of sound in the medium. For example:

Mach 1 = speed of sound

Mach 2 = twice the speed of sound

Mach 3 = three times the speed of sound

A sonic boom typically occurs when an object exceeds Mach 1 (the speed of sound), but the intensity of the boom increases with the Mach number.

Summary:

A sonic boom is the shockwave generated when an object travels faster than the speed of sound.

The phenomenon results in a loud, abrupt noise that is often compared to a thunderclap or explosion.

It occurs when an object breaks the sound barrier (Mach 1) and creates a pressure wave that expands outward.

Sonic booms can cause physical damage, such as breaking windows, and are a significant concern for supersonic flight over populated areas.

Sound depends on many things.

1. Pitch
2. Loudness
3. Quality of musical sound

Pitch:-

We can distinguish between a man's voice and a women's voice of the same loudness even without seeing them. this is because a man's voice and a women's voice differ in pitch.

A man's voice is flat having a low pitch, whereas a women's voice is shrill having a high pitch.

Pitch is that characteristic of sound by which we can distinguished between different sound of the same loudness.

Pitch of the sound depends upon the frequency of the vibration.

Pitch of the sound is directly proportional to its frequency.

loudness:-

The loudness of sound is a measure of the sound energy reaching the ear per second.

Loudness of the sound depends on the amplitude of sound wave.

The greater the amplitude of sound wave , louder the sound will be.

The S.I unit of loudness of sound is decibel. ' dB '.

The softest sound which human ears can here is said to have a loudness of zero decibel.

The loudness of sound of people talking quietly is about 65 decibel.

Quality of musical sound:-

The quality of musical sound refers to the unique characteristics that allow us to distinguish one sound from another, even when the pitch and loudness are the same. This quality is often described by the term timbre (or tone color), which is the distinctive "color" or "texture" of a sound. Timbre allows us to differentiate between the sound of a violin, a piano, or a human voice, even if they are all playing the same note at the same volume. The physical properties of the sound source—such as its shape, size, and the materials from which it's made—have a direct influence on its timbre.

Reflection of sound

Reflection of sound occurs when sound waves encounter a surface or boundary that they cannot pass through, causing the waves to bounce back into the medium. The phenomenon is similar to the reflection of light, but with sound waves, the principles involve the interaction between the sound wave and the surface or object it meets. Reflection plays an important role in both natural and engineered acoustic environments and is responsible for phenomena like echoes and reverberation.

Basic Principle of Reflection:

The reflection of sound is governed by the law of reflection, which states that:

Angle of Incidence = Angle of Reflection

This means that the angle at which the sound wave strikes the surface (the incident angle) will be equal to the angle at which the sound wave reflects off the surface (the reflected angle). The sound wave is reflected back into the same medium (like air) at a consistent angle, and this interaction typically occurs at solid surfaces like walls, buildings, or cliffs.

Factors Affecting the Reflection of Sound:

- Surface Properties:

Hard, smooth surfaces (like walls, metal, or glass) are excellent reflectors of sound because they do not absorb much of the sound energy. The reflected sound is often strong and clear.

Soft, irregular surfaces (like carpets, curtains, or foam panels) absorb more sound energy and therefore produce less reflection. These materials tend to reduce echo and reverberation, contributing to a more controlled acoustic environment.

- Distance and Shape of the Reflecting Surface:

The distance between the sound source and the reflective surface affects the time it takes for the reflected sound to return. This time difference is critical in distinguishing between an echo and reverberation.

The shape of the surface also matters. Curved surfaces, such as domed ceilings or parabolic reflectors, can concentrate sound in specific directions, leading to effects like focusing sound or creating hot spots of sound.

- Frequency of the Sound:

Low-frequency sounds (bass) tend to diffuse more when reflected, and they don't produce clear echoes. They are more likely to be absorbed by the environment, especially in large rooms.

High-frequency sounds (treble) are more directional and are typically reflected more clearly, producing sharper, more noticeable echoes.

Phenomena Due to Sound Reflection:

- Echo:

An echo is the reflection of sound that is heard after a delay. For an echo to be distinctly heard, the sound wave must travel a sufficient distance to the reflecting surface and then return to the listener. The minimum distance for an echo to be heard is typically around 17 meters (about 56 feet) in air, though this can vary depending on the medium and environment.

Echoes are commonly experienced in large, open spaces such as mountains, valleys, or large empty buildings. A classic example is shouting near a cliff and hearing your voice come back to you after a short delay.

- Reverberation:

Reverberation occurs when sound waves are reflected off multiple surfaces in a room or space, causing the sound to persist and blend with new sounds. Unlike echoes, which are distinct and separated in time, reverberation is the continuation of sound due to the repeated reflections from various surfaces. This effect is especially important in concert halls and auditoriums, where architects design the space to have specific reflection patterns to enhance acoustic quality.

In large, reflective spaces like cathedrals or theaters, reverberation can create a rich, full sound. However, excessive reverberation can make speech or music unclear, which is why good acoustic design is necessary to balance reflections.

- Sonar and Echo Location:

Sonar (Sound Navigation and Ranging) is a technology that relies on the reflection of sound waves to detect objects underwater. In sonar systems, a sound wave (often called a "ping") is emitted, and the time it takes for the wave to reflect off an object and return to the receiver is measured. This helps in determining the distance and location of objects like submarines, fish, or the ocean floor.

Echolocation, used by animals such as bats and dolphins, is a biological form of sound reflection. These animals emit sound waves, and by listening to the echoes that bounce off objects, they can navigate their environment or locate prey.

Applications of Sound Reflection:

- Acoustic Design and Architecture:

The reflection of sound is carefully managed in architectural acoustics to create spaces with optimal sound clarity. Concert halls, theaters, and recording studios often use reflective materials and strategically placed surfaces to ensure that sound is reflected in a way that enhances auditory experience without producing unwanted echoes.

In auditorium design, the placement of reflectors on ceilings and walls can help distribute sound evenly across the entire space, ensuring that every seat in the hall hears a balanced sound.

- Noise Control:

Reflection of sound is also a factor in noise pollution. In urban areas, sound reflects off buildings and other structures, amplifying noise levels. This is why areas with dense buildings often experience higher levels of noise.

To combat this, soundproofing materials like acoustic panels, barriers, and insulation are used to absorb or redirect sound waves, reducing unwanted reflections.

- Reflection in the Atmosphere:

The reflection of sound can also be influenced by the atmospheric conditions. For instance, sound waves travel faster in warmer air and slower in cooler air, which can cause sound to bend or reflect differently depending on the temperature gradient between different layers of air. This phenomenon is known as refraction, but it can combine with reflection to alter how sound is perceived over large distances.

Conclusion:

The reflection of sound plays a vital role in shaping how we experience sound in various environments. Whether it's the distinct echo heard in the mountains, the reverberation enhancing the acoustics in a concert hall, or the use of sound reflection in technologies like sonar, understanding how sound waves interact with surfaces is essential in many fields, from architecture to navigation. Proper management of sound reflection allows for better control of sound quality, improving communication, music performance, and even safety in certain applications.

CHAPTER SEVEN

Light

Introduction

Reflection of light is the phenomenon of natural that plays with the behaviour of light. In the further of the post we will discuss about reflection and some common examples of reflection of light in more depth ways. But before we procced we have to first know a little about reflection and how it happens in any surface weather it is rough, smooth, and curve. So let's start with what is reflection.

What is reflection of light?

Reflection is the natural phenomenon of light that seperate the light waves to go through a straight line. Means it is due to the reflection that a beam of light changes its path.

In other words the bouncing back of light wave in the same medium when strikes with any surfaces weather it is plane, curve or rough.

For example, you can see in the above fig. That a tree get reflection in water. It is happens as follows: when the rays of light falls on the tree then tree becomes luminous object and a luminous object easily get reflected in a smooth surface. Here the smooth surface is water. That's why a virtual image of tree formed in the water.

Luminous object is that object which has its own light. Means the object should be glowing or have some light in itself.

To understand the reflection of light in more detail lets see the another definition.

When a source or an object emitting the rays of light and if these rays of light get touched with any regular or irregular surface then the rays of light get bounced back and spread in all directions. Some of rays get back on its initial path, some are get diffused, some are followed the laws of reflection.

In the above definition of reflection of light. We have used many terms like regular, irregular, diffusion, and laws of reflection. So what was that terms means. because examples of reflection will not be understand if the concept of these terms will not clear. So before we start examples of reflection let's understand all the above terms one by one.

Types of reflection of light

There are many types of reflection of light in daily life. But we discuss only most common and relevant types that is,

- Regular reflection of light
- Irregular or diffusion of light
- Multiple reflection of light.

1. Regular reflection of light

If the rays of light fall on a smooth surface and light waves get reflected in only one direction then it will be the regular reflection of light.

Regular reflection of light can also be defined as the light waves falls on a polished surface and get reflected in such a way that all the light waves will be parallel to each other.

2. Irregular or diffuse reflection of light

If a ray of light falls on a rough surface then after reflection light waves get diffuse in all directions.

Irregular reflection of light can also be defined as when teh rays of light fall on a surface that is not polished then after reflection it will bounce back in the same medium but not each rays will be parallel to each other.

3. Multiple reflection of light

When a rays of light fall on a surface weather it is rough or polished and the surface are placed with many other polished or rough surfaces in such a way that after reflection of light from one surface the reflected rays fall on the other surface and again reflected rays of second surface falls on the third surface and so on. Then these types of reflection is called multiple reflection of light.

In short way multiple reflection of light can be defined as when a ray of light falls on surface1 and after reflection the reflected ray of surface1 falls on a surface 2 and so on. Then these types of reflection called multiple reflection of light.

See the below fig. to understand the multiple reflection of light.

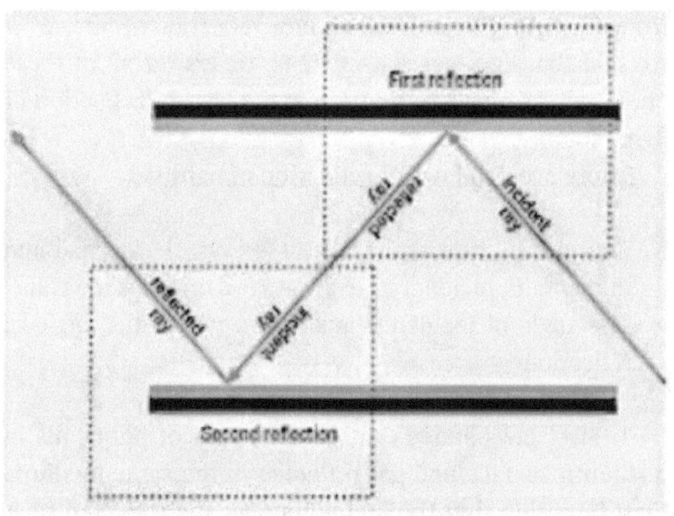

In the above fig. We can see there are two surfaces named first reflection and second reflection. When a ray of light incident on the first surface it get reflected and falls on the second surface. Now the reflected ray which is falls on the second surface becomes a incident ray of second surface. So that after reflection from second surface it will again become reflected ray.

You can see the examples of multiple reflection of light in your daily life. Like if you placed a two mirror in such a way that if we bring an object between them then the image will formed in both the mirror. The best example is the mirror placed in hair cut store 'salon'.

Laws of reflection of light

We have understood the phenomena of refraction of light. Now we will try to understand how reflection occurs. Why we said that light get reflected? So to answer all of these questions. We have to first know the laws of reflection of light.

There are two laws of reflection of light.

- The incidents rays, the reflected rays, the normal and the point of incidence are always lies on the same plane.
- The angle of incidence is always equal to the angle of reflection.

1. First laws states that if some rays of light falls in a smooth surface and get reflected in the same medium. First laws said that the incidents rays, the reflected rays, the normal and point of incidence are all lies on that smooth surface.

2. Second laws state that when incident rays falls on a plane surface and get reflected then the angle made by incident rays with normal is equal to the angle made by reflected rays with normal.

Please note that:- The incident rays makes $\angle i$ and the reflected rays makes $\angle r$. So that $\angle i = \angle r$.

Now, after knowing some useful concepts of reflection of light. Its time to go through examples.

Examples of reflection of light

9 most commonly seen examples of reflection of light in daily life with naked eyes.

1. Reflection of light in mirror.
2. Reflection of light in spherical mirror.
3. Reflection of light in water pool.
4. Reflection of light on polished surface.
5. Object seen due to reflection of light.
6. Glowing of stars.
7. Lighting of moon at night.
8. Reflection from luminous object.
9. Reflection from non-luminous objects.

Let's discuss all of the above examples of reflection of light which we can observe in our day to day life.

1. Reflection of light in mirror.

Reflection of light in mirror is the best example of reflection of light. In plane polished surface of the mirror glass the light wave reflect so well that it follows both the laws of reflection of light.

In plane mirror, regular reflection takes place. Because the particles present on the surface of the plane mirror are faced in only one direction. That's why a plane mirror shows a regular reflection of light.

But if you talk about the rough surface. The particles on the surface of the rough part are faced in many directions. That's why irregular reflection of light takes place in rough surface.

If you see the surface of the plane mirror through a microscope then you will find that the particles are faced in only one direction.

Now, let's know how a plane mirror reflects all the rays in only one directions.

So the answer is, when a beam of light falls on a smooth surface like the surface of the plane mirror. Then due to the particles faced in one particular directions, all the light waves get reflected on that direction.

See the given below fig. to learn how a plane mirror shows regular reflection of light.

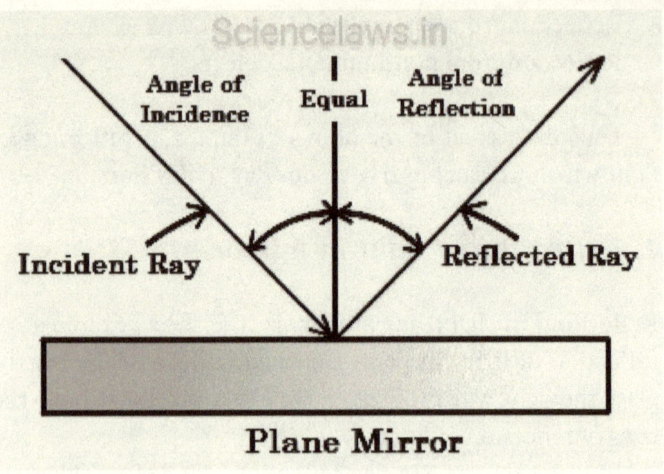

In the above fig. An incident rays falls on the surface of a plane mirror and reflect. Reflection takes place in such a way that, incident rays and reflected rays makes angle of incidence and angle of reflection respectively.

Both angle of incidence and angle of reflection are equal. Because it follows the laws of reflection of light. See fig.

2. Reflection of light in spherical mirror.

After the discussion of reflection of light in plane mirror. Its time to take some knowledge about reflection in spherical mirror.

If we talk about spherical mirror. Then it is a part of a complete sphere. In simple words take a spherical ball and cut it into two pieces equally. The each cut part is like a spherical mirror.

Inner part of the cutted spherical ball is called concave. And outer surface of the cutted spherical ball called convex.

Here we will learn both, reflection in concave and reflection in convex.

Reflection of light in spherical mirror is same as in plane mirror. But it is not that simple. To understand the reflection in spherical mirror. We have to learn reflection in concave and convex mirror.

Reflection in concave mirror

As we discussed just now that reflection of light in concave mirror is same as reflection of light in plane mirror.

In a concave mirror, reflection can takes place in any part of the mirror. But it should be from inside. Because concave mirror is polished from outside. See the given fig.

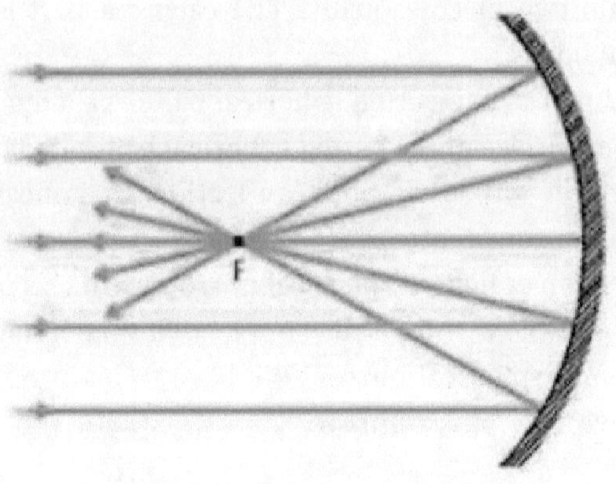

In concave mirror a regular reflection of light takes place only when if it follows certain conditions. These are some conditions which must have to follow for regular reflection in concave mirror.

If the light waves are parallel to the principal axis then it the reflected rays will pass through the focus point (F).

If light waves passes through the focus then the reflected rays become parallel to the principal axis.

If the incident rays are align with the principal axis then reflected rays will returns to the same path.

As you can see in the above fig. that there are two light waves on upper side of the principal axis and two in the downward direction. All of them strikes with the inner part of the concave mirror. And after the reflection all the waves passed through the focus point. because it follows the laws of reflection of light.

Reflection in convex mirror

In convex mirror, the light waves are are also get reflected and follows the laws of reflection of light. But the reflection takes places from the outside of the mirror. Because in convex mirror, inner side is polished and outer side is shiny. That's why reflection takes place from outside.

In a convex mirror, reflection can takes place in any part of the mirror. But it should be from outside. Because convex mirror is polished from outside. See the given fig.

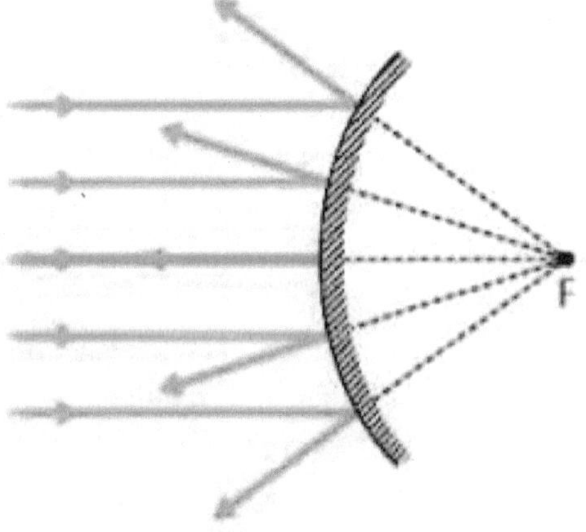

In convex mirror also a regular reflection of light takes place only when if it follows certain conditions. These are some conditions which must have to follow for regular reflection in convex mirror.

If the light waves are parallel to the principal axis then it the reflected rays will pass through the focus point (F).

If light waves passes through the focus then the reflected rays become parallel to the principal axis.

If the incident rays are align with the principal axis then reflected rays will returns to the same path.

As you can see in the above fig. that there are two light waves on upper side of the principal axis and two in the downward direction. All of them strikes with the inner part of the convex mirror. And after the reflection all the waves passed through the focus point. because it follows the laws of reflection of light.

3. Reflection of light in water pool.

Reflection can also takes place in water. If you observed that, if anyone see into the water. Then an image of that object or person get virtual into the surface of the water. How this happens?

As we know reflection can takes place on both the surface. Weather it is regular or irregular. A water surface is quite regular so that when the rays of light falls on the surface of the water then some of the rays follows laws of reflection and some are not.

4. Reflection of light on polished surface.

As we know that reflection on the surface of the mirror is the best example of reflection of light. Because a mirror surface is also polished.

So on any highly polished surface, reflection can easily takes place. The best example of reflection of light on polished surface will be , reflection in stainless steel.

In vessels or stainless steel, reflection takes place. Because stainless steel has also a polished surface.

5. Object seen due to reflection.

Do you know, why we can see the objects in our surroundings? Why you are able to read this article.

The answers are due to reflection of light. But how? Let's understand.

When an object placed in the light room or to any other sources of light then it emit some source of light from itself and when these emitted light waves enters in our eyes. So that we are able to see the objects.

To seeing an object there one important thing is light. Without light it is not possible to see an object through our neked eyes.

How reflection is responsible for seeing an object?

Let suppose an object is placed in the dark room. Where there is no any sources of light.

Now placed a light bulb ? in the room. Now you can see the object very easily. But how this happens? This happens due to the reflection of light through object. Explain.

When you being a light source closer to the object. And we know that a glowing bulb emit a tons of light rays.

And when these light wave get reflected from the objects placed on that room and when that reflected rays enters in our eyes, it forms a virtual and inverted image in the retina.

After that mind correct that image and recognise. That's why we are able to see the objects in our surroundings.

6. Glowing of stars.

At night, sky are full of stars. Some of the star ??? glow brightly and some are not. But have you ever think why these stars are always seen glowing?

Starts glow because it is luminous object. But is that's it. Is this answer ok? No my dear friends. No way.

Starts are glowing because of their own light emitting from itself. But how we able to see it?

The answer is just because of the reflection of light emitted from stars. Learn how?

The glowing stars are always emitting light waves. And when these light waves travel through space and come near the earth's surface. Then it strikes with the atmosphere of the earth and at that time some of the light waves get returns into the space. But some are reflected towards the centre of the earth.

That's the reason we can see the glowing stars even it is far from us.

7. Lighting of moon at night.

Lighting of moon is also an example of reflection of light. Moon is lighting not because of it has own light. It is glowing because it reflects the light waves coming from the sun.

As we know moon is non-luminous objects. Perhaps it is glowing due to reflection of light.

Reflection takes place on the surface of the moon. And due to the irregular surface, when Sun light touches it's ground, the light waves get diffuse and some of the light enters on the earth through atmosphere.

8. Reflection from luminous objects.

Luminous object emit light waves from itself. And when these light waves collide with any other objects or non-luminous objects. Then it makes us to see that non-luminous objects.

So due to the reflection or we can say, with the help of reflection phenomenon a non-luminous objects can be seen

In other words, due to reflection of light a non-luminous objects becomes luminous object and can emit light waves.

9. Reflection from non-luminous objects.

As we just discussed above that a reflection of light makes a non-luminous objects into a luminous object.

So it is also clear that non-luminous objects emit light due to reflection and make things visible.

Application of reflection of light.

These are the some applications of reflection of light.

- Microscope works on the application of reflection of light. Because in microscope there are some small mirror piece used to see the objects.
- Kaleidoscope also works on the principal of reflection of light.

- The best application of reflection of light is the working of telescope. In inside of the telescope reflection takes place.
- In cars side mirror.

CHAPTER EIGHT

Human Eye And Colorful World

1. The Human Eye

<u>**Structure of the Human Eye:**</u>

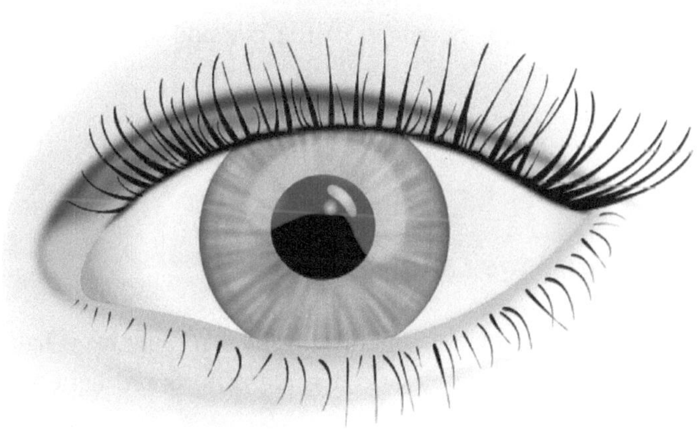

Original Human Eye

1. Cornea: Transparent, curved surface that refracts light entering the eye.
2. Pupil: The black circular opening in the center of the eye that controls the amount of light entering the eye. The size of the pupil is controlled by the iris.
3. Iris: The colored part of the eye that controls the size of the pupil.
4. Lens: A transparent, flexible structure behind the pupil that focuses light onto the retina.
5. Retina: The light-sensitive layer at the back of the eye, where images are formed. It has photoreceptor cells, rods (for black and white vision) and cones (for color vision).
6. Optic Nerve: Transmits the visual information from the retina to the brain.
7. Aqueous and Vitreous Humors: Fluids in the eye that help maintain the shape of the eye and assist in light refraction.

Color and the Color of Objects

The color of an object depends on the wavelengths of light it reflects. For example, a red apple reflects red light and absorbs other colors.

Objects appear different colors based on the light they absorb or reflect.

The Rainbow

A rainbow is formed when light is dispersed by water droplets in the atmosphere. The sunlight is refracted, reflected, and dispersed, creating a spectrum of colors in the sky.

Applications of Refraction

Eyeglasses: Use of lenses to correct vision defects like myopia and hypermetropia.

Prisms: Used to study the dispersion of light and to create rainbows.

Optical Instruments: Microscopes, telescopes, and cameras all rely on the principles of light refraction to form clear images.

Basic Structure of Human Eye

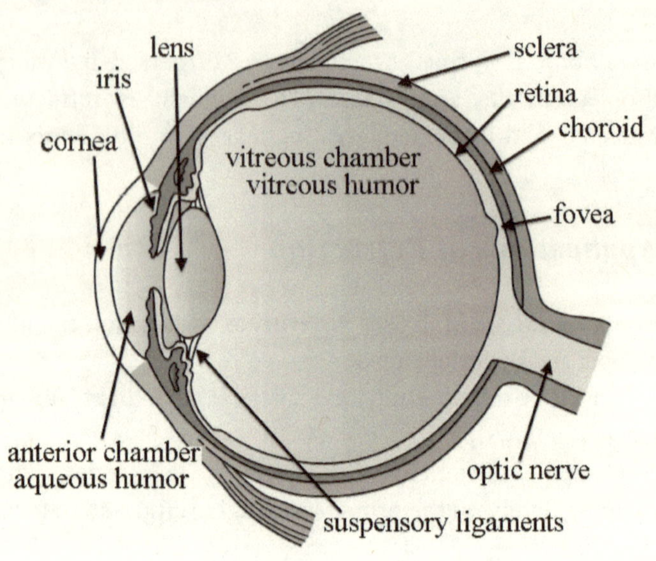

Inner Srtucture of Human Eye

Working of the Human Eye:

Light enters the eye through the cornea, passing through the pupil and lens.

The lens focuses the light onto the retina, where the image is formed.

The image is inverted and transmitted to the brain via the optic nerve, which interprets it as a right-side-up image.

Accommodation:

The process by which the eye changes its focal length to focus on objects at different distances.

The ciliary muscles control the shape of the eye's lens. When looking at nearby objects, the lens becomes thicker;

for distant objects, it becomes thinner.

Defects of the Eye:

Myopia (Nearsightedness): A defect where a person can see nearby objects clearly but has difficulty seeing distant objects. It is corrected with concave lenses.

Hypermetropia (Farsightedness): A defect where a person can see distant objects clearly but struggles with nearby objects. It is corrected with convex lenses.

Astigmatism: A defect where the cornea or lens has an irregular shape, causing blurred vision. It is corrected with cylindrical lenses.

Presbyopia: A condition that occurs with age, where the eye's ability to focus on near objects decreases due to a stiffening of the lens. It can be corrected with bifocal lenses.

Questions Based On Unit And Measurement

Here are some Multiple Choice Questions (MCQs) for the Chapter "Units and Measurement" for Class 9 Physics:

MCQs: Unit and Measurement

Which of the following is the SI unit of length?

a) Meter (m)
b) Centimeter (cm)
c) Kilometer (km)
d) Foot (ft)

Answer: a) Meter (m)

Which of the following is NOT a fundamental quantity?

a) Length
b) Time
c) Mass
d) Velocity

Answer: d) Velocity

The measurement of mass in kilograms is an example of which type of unit?

a) Derived Unit
b) Fundamental Unit
c) Subordinate Unit
d) Both a and b

Answer: b) Fundamental Unit

What is the SI unit of time?

a) Second (s)
b) Minute (min)
c) Hour (h)
d) Day

Answer: a) Second (s)

Which of the following is the correct SI unit of velocity?

a) m/s
b) m/s^2
c) km/h
d) m

Answer: a) m/s

The prefix 'kilo-' means:

a) 1000
b) 100
c) 100000
d) 1000,000

Answer: a) 1000

The numerical value of a physical quantity is always dependent on:

a) The units used for measurement
b) The measurement instrument
c) The temperature
d) The environment

Answer: a) The units used for measurement

Which of the following is a derived unit in SI?

a) Meter
b) Kilogram
c) Newton
d) Second

Answer: c) Newton

What is the fundamental quantity that is measured in kilograms?

a) Mass
b) Length
c) Temperature
d) Time

Answer: a) Mass

The unit "Newton" is used to measure:

a) Mass

b) Force
c) Energy
d) Speed

Answer: b) Force

How many meters are there in 1 kilometer?

a) 100
b) 1000
c) 10
d) 10000

Answer: b) 1000

Which of the following is the correct way to express 0.00045 m in scientific notation?

a) 4.5×10^4 m
b) 4.5×10^{-4} m
c) 4.5×10^{-3} m
d) 45×10^{-5} m

Answer: b) 4.5×10^{-4} m

The process of expressing a number in scientific notation is called:

a) Rounding
b) Estimation
c) Normalization
d) Standardization

Answer: c) Normalization

What is the unit of area in SI?

a) m
b) m^2
c) cm
d) m^3

Answer: b) m^2

Which of the following is the correct SI unit of density?

a) kg/m^3
b) kg/m

c) m^2/s
d) kg/s

Answer: a) kg/m^3

What does the SI prefix "centi-" represent?

a) 1/100
b) 100
c) 1/1000
d) 10

Answer: a) 1/100

Which of the following measurements is most precise?

a) 2.34 m
b) 2.3 m
c) 2 m
d) 2.345 m

Answer: d) 2.345 m

The term "accuracy" in measurement refers to:

a) The closeness of a measured value to the true value
b) The repeatability of measurements
c) The size of the measuring instrument
d) The ability to estimate values

Answer: a) The closeness of a measured value to the true value

The numerical value of the physical quantity should be:

a) Always positive
b) Always negative
c) Always zero
d) Can be positive or negative, depending on the quantity

Answer: d) Can be positive or negative, depending on the quantity

What is the SI unit of the electric current?

a) Ampere (A)
b) Coulomb (C)
c) Volt (V)

d) Ohm (Ω)

Answer: a) Ampere (A)

These questions cover the essential concepts of the "Units and Measurement" chapter, testing students' understanding of both the theoretical and practical aspects of physical quantities and units.

Question Based On Motion

Here are some Multiple Choice Questions (MCQs), Short Answer Questions, and Numerical Problems based on the "Motion" chapter for Class 9 Physics:

MCQs (Multiple Choice Questions)

What is the SI unit of speed?

a) m/s^2
b) m
c) m/s
d) km/h
Answer: c) m/s

If an object is moving with uniform speed along a straight line, its velocity is:

a) Constant
b) Zero
c) Increasing
d) Decreasing
Answer: a) Constant

The distance-time graph of an object moving with uniform velocity is:

a) A straight line with a slope
b) A curve
c) A vertical line
d) A horizontal line
Answer: a) A straight line with a slope

Which of the following quantities is a vector?

a) Speed
b) Distance
c) Displacement

d) Time

Answer: c) Displacement

The slope of a velocity-time graph gives:

a) Displacement

b) Acceleration

c) Speed

d) Distance

Answer: b) Acceleration

If an object is said to be in uniform circular motion, then the direction of its velocity:

a) Changes continuously

b) Does not change

c) Becomes zero

d) Remains constant

Answer: a) Changes continuously

A car travels a distance of 100 meters in 10 seconds. What is its speed?

a) 10 m/s

b) 5 m/s

c) 100 m/s

d) 1000 m/s

Answer: b) 10 m/s

The rate of change of velocity is called:

a) Speed

b) Distance

c) Acceleration

d) Displacement

Answer: c) Acceleration

The area under a velocity-time graph represents:

a) Speed

b) Acceleration

c) Distance

d) Displacement

Answer: d) Displacement

A body moves with uniform velocity. Its acceleration is:

a) Zero

b) Positive

c) Negative

d) Infinite

Answer: a) Zero

Short Answer Questions

What is the difference between distance and displacement?

Answer:

Distance is the total path length covered by an object, irrespective of the direction. It is a scalar quantity.

Displacement is the shortest straight-line distance between the initial and final positions of the object, along with the direction. It is a vector quantity.

What do you understand by "uniform motion"? Give an example.

Answer:

Uniform motion refers to the motion in which an object covers equal distances in equal intervals of time, regardless of the time duration.

Example: A car moving at a constant speed on a straight road.

What is acceleration? How is it different from velocity?

Answer:

Acceleration is the rate of change of velocity of an object with respect to time. It is a vector quantity and is measured in m/s^2.

Velocity is the rate of change of displacement, and it has both magnitude and direction. Acceleration is the change in velocity over time, while velocity is the rate of displacement.

What is the significance of the slope of a distance-time graph?

Answer:

The slope of a distance-time graph represents the speed or velocity of the object. A constant slope means uniform motion, while a changing slope indicates non-uniform motion.

Explain what is meant by "non-uniform motion" and give an example.

Answer:

Non-uniform motion refers to the motion of an object when it covers unequal distances in equal intervals of time.

Example: A car moving with varying speeds in traffic.

Here are 20 numerical questions based on the Motion chapter for Class 9 CBSE:

1. A car starts from rest and accelerates uniformly at 2 m/s^2 for 5 seconds. Find its final velocity.
2. A ball is thrown vertically upwards with a velocity of 10 m/s. Calculate the maximum height it reaches.
3. A train is moving with a velocity of 36 km/h. Convert its velocity into m/s.
4. A motorcycle starts from rest and reaches a velocity of 20 m/s in 10 seconds. What is its acceleration?
5. A stone is dropped from the top of a building. How long will it take to reach the ground if the height of the building is 45 m? (Assume g=9.8 m/s2g = 9.8 \, \text{m/s}^2)
6. A car accelerates from 10 m/s to 30 m/s in 5 seconds.

Find its acceleration.

7. A cyclist moves with a constant speed of 12 m/s. How far will the cyclist travel in 15 seconds?
8. A ball is thrown vertically downwards with an initial velocity of 5 m/s. Calculate its velocity after 3 seconds.
9. A train accelerates uniformly from 0 to 72 km/h in 10 minutes. What is its acceleration in m/s^2?
10. A car is moving with an initial velocity of 20 m/s. It decelerates at 2 m/s^2. Find the time it will take to stop.
11. A body moves with a constant velocity of 5 m/s. How much distance will it cover in 10 seconds?
12. A car accelerates at 4 m/s^2 for 3 seconds. What is the distance traveled during this time?
13. A stone is thrown vertically upwards with an initial speed of 15 m/s. Find the time taken to reach the highest point.
14. A car is moving at a speed of 36 km/h. It accelerates at 2 m/s^2 for 10 seconds. What is its final speed?
15. A runner runs at a speed of 9 m/s for 100 meters. How much time does it take to complete the distance?
16. A bus starts from rest and moves with a constant acceleration of 1 m/s^2. What will be the velocity after 20 seconds?
17. A bullet is fired vertically upward with an initial speed of 50 m/s. Find the maximum height it reaches.
18. A train moves with a uniform velocity of 72 km/h for 20 minutes. How far does it travel?
19. A person throws a ball vertically upwards with an initial speed of 12 m/s. Calculate the total time the ball remains in the air.
20. A car moving at a constant velocity of 18 m/s takes 10 seconds to pass a bridge. If the length of the bridge is 150 meters, what is the speed of the car in km/h?

These questions cover a wide range of concepts in motion and can be solved using the three equations of motion and basic kinematic principles.

<u>Answer:-</u>

Here are the one-word answers to the 20 numerical questions based on the Motion chapter for Class 9 CBSE:

1. 10 m/s
2. 5 m
3. 10 m/s
4. 2 m/s^2
5. 3 seconds
6. 4 m/s^2
7. 180 meters
8. 29.4 m/s
9. 0.2 m/s^2
10. 10 seconds
11. 50 meters
12. 18 meters
13. 1.5 seconds
14. 40 m/s
15. 11.11 seconds
16. 20 m/s
17. 127.5 meters
18. 2400 meters
19. 2.4 seconds
20. 64.8 km/h

Here are 20 more challenging numerical questions based on the Motion chapter for Class 9 CBSE:

1. A body starts from rest and accelerates uniformly at 4 m/s^2. Find the time it will take to cover a distance of 100 meters.
2. A car is moving with a velocity of 15 m/s and decelerates at 3 m/s^2. How much time will it take to stop?
3. A stone is thrown vertically upwards with a velocity of 20 m/s. How high will it rise before coming to rest?
4. A cyclist accelerates from 5 m/s to 15 m/s in 10 seconds. Find the distance covered during this time.
5. A car moving at 72 km/h accelerates uniformly to 108 km/h in 5 minutes. Calculate the acceleration in m/s^2.
6. A stone is thrown vertically upwards with an initial velocity of 30 m/s. How long will it take to reach the highest point?
7. A ball is dropped from a height of 80 meters. How much time will it take to hit the ground? (Take g=9.8 m/s2g = 9.8 {m/s}^2)
8. A car is traveling with a constant speed of 72 km/h. How long will it take to travel a distance of 540 meters?
9. A train accelerates from rest to 54 km/h in 20 seconds. What is its acceleration?
10. A body moves with an initial velocity of 10 m/s and accelerates at 2 m/s^2 for 6 seconds. Find its final velocity and displacement.
11. A car is moving at 20 m/s. It starts decelerating at 2 m/s^2. How far will the car travel before coming to rest?
12. A ball is thrown upwards with a velocity of 15 m/s. Calculate the time taken to return to the ground.
13. A bus accelerates from 15 m/s to 25 m/s in 10 seconds. What is the acceleration?
14. A stone is dropped from a height of 100 meters. What will be its velocity just before hitting the ground?

15. A body is moving with a velocity of 30 m/s and decelerates at 5 m/s^2. How much time will it take to come to rest?
16. A motorboat starts from rest and accelerates at 2 m/s^2 for 10 seconds. What is its final velocity and distance traveled?
17. A car accelerates from 10 m/s to 30 m/s in 15 seconds. Find the distance covered during this time.
18. A stone is thrown vertically upwards with an initial speed of 25 m/s. Find the time taken to reach the highest point and the maximum height.
19. A train moving at a velocity of 20 m/s accelerates at 1.5 m/s^2 for 30 seconds. Find the final velocity and the distance covered during this time.
20. A ball is dropped from a height of 45 meters. How much time will it take to hit the ground? (Take g=9.8 m/s2g = 9.8{m/s}^2)

These questions require careful application of the equations of motion and may involve multiple steps or concepts like conversion of units, free fall, and deceleration.

<u>Here are the one-word answers to the 20 challenging questions based on the Motion chapter for Class 9 CBSE:</u>

1. 5 seconds
2. 5 seconds
3. 20 meters
4. 100 meters
5. 0.2 m/s^2
6. 3.06 seconds
7. 4.04 seconds
8. 22.5 seconds

9. 2.5 m/s^2
10. 22 m/s, 72 meters
11. 100 meters
12. 3.06 seconds
13. 1 m/s^2
14. 40 m/s
15. 6 seconds
16. 20 m/s, 100 meters
17. 300 meters
18. 2.5 seconds, 31.25 meters
19. 65 m/s, 450 meters
20. 3.03 seconds

These answers are derived using kinematic equations and basic motion principles.

Question Based On Force And Laws Of Motion

Here are multiple-choice questions (MCQs) based on Force and Laws of Motion for Class 9 CBSE:

MCQs on Force and Laws of Motion

1.Which of the following is the unit of force?

a) Joule
b) Watt
c) Newton
d) Pascal

2.Newton's First Law of Motion is also known as:

a) Law of Inertia
b) Law of Acceleration
c) Law of Action and Reaction
d) Law of Gravity

3.What is the SI unit of acceleration?

a) m/s
b) m/s^2
c) kg/m^2
d) N

4.Which of the following quantities is a vector quantity?

a) Speed
b) Distance
c) Velocity
d) Time

5.An object of mass 10 kg is moving with an acceleration of 2 m/s^2. What is the force acting on the object?

a) 5 N
b) 10 N
c) 20 N

d) 30 N

6. Which of the following statements is correct according to Newton's Third Law of Motion?

a) Action and reaction forces act on the same object.
b) Action and reaction forces are always unequal.
c) Action and reaction forces act on different objects.
d) Action and reaction forces are always in the same direction.

7. If a person is standing on a scale inside an elevator moving upwards, what force will the scale measure?

a) Weight of the person
b) The net force on the person
c) Normal force
d) Apparent weight

8. What is the acceleration of an object in free fall due to gravity near the Earth's surface?

a) $9.8 \, m/s^2$
b) $10 \, m/s^2$
c) 9.8 m/s
d) 10 m/s

9. Which of the following is an example of an external force acting on an object?

a) Gravitational pull
b) Tension in a rope
c) Friction between surfaces
d) A person pushing a car

10. A car of mass 1000 kg accelerates from 0 to 20 m/s in 10 seconds. What is the force exerted by the car?

a) 5000 N
b) 2000 N
c) 1000 N
d) 4000 N

11. The force that resists the relative motion of two surfaces in contact is called:

a) Tension
b) Friction
c) Gravity
d) Normal force

12. According to Newton's Second Law of Motion, force is directly proportional to:

a) Mass
b) Acceleration
c) Both mass and velocity
d) Acceleration and velocity

13. In which of the following cases does the total momentum remain constant?

a) When two objects collide in an inelastic collision
b) When two objects collide in an elastic collision
c) When a ball falls to the ground
d) When a car accelerates on a road

14. If a body is acted upon by a net force, it will:

a) Remain at rest
b) Move with constant velocity
c) Accelerate
d) None of the above

15. Which of the following is an example of Newton's Third Law of Motion?

a) A rocket moves upwards by expelling gas downwards.
b) A moving car slows down due to friction.
c) An object remains stationary unless acted upon by a force.
d) A ball accelerates when a force is applied.

16. What happens to the acceleration of an object if the net force acting on it is doubled while its mass remains

constant?

a) The acceleration is halved.
b) The acceleration remains the same.
c) The acceleration is doubled.
d) The acceleration becomes four times greater.

17. In the case of a frictionless surface, an object in motion will:

a) Eventually stop
b) Continue moving indefinitely
c) Accelerate continuously
d) Decelerate gradually

18. The unit of momentum is:

a) kg
b) m/s
c) N·s
d) kg·m/s

19. Which of the following is not a contact force?

a) Friction
b) Tension
c) Gravitational force
d) Normal force

20. Which of the following examples violates Newton's First Law of Motion?

a) A book resting on a table
b) A car moving at constant velocity
c) A car accelerating on a road
d) An object in free fall near the Earth's surface

Answers:

1. c) Newton
2. a) Law of Inertia
3. b) m/s^2
4. c) Velocity

5. c) 20 N
6. c) Action and reaction forces act on different objects.
7. d) Apparent weight
8. a) 9.8 m/s^2
9. d) A person pushing a car
10. b) 2000 N
11. b) Friction
12. b) Acceleration
13. b) When two objects collide in an elastic collision
14. c) Accelerate
15. a) A rocket moves upwards by expelling gas downwards.
16. c) The acceleration is doubled.
17. b) Continue moving indefinitely
18. d) kg·m/s
19. c) Gravitational force
20. c) A car accelerating on a road

These questions are designed to test your understanding of the concepts of force, laws of motion, and momentum.

Here are 20 one-word questions based on Force and Laws of Motion for Class 9 CBSE:

1. What is the SI unit of force?
2. Which law explains inertia?
3. What is the unit of acceleration?
4. Which quantity is described by both magnitude and direction?
5. What force opposes motion between two surfaces?
6. What is the unit of momentum?
7. What type of force is responsible for motion in a rocket?

8. Which force keeps objects in orbit around the Earth?
9. What does Newton's second law relate to?
10. What is the reaction force when a swimmer pushes water backward?
11. What law states that force is equal to mass times acceleration?
12. What is the acceleration due to gravity?
13. What is the term for the force that resists the motion of a vehicle on the road?
14. What type of collision conserves both momentum and kinetic energy?
15. What quantity is conserved during a collision?
16. What is the force that acts at a distance without contact?
17. What term describes the motion of an object without changing speed or direction?
18. What is the force called that pulls objects toward the Earth?
19. What force makes objects fall towards the ground?
20. What does Newton's third law state?

These questions are aimed at testing your understanding of fundamental concepts related to force and motion.

Here are the one-word answers to the previous questions:

1. Newton
2. Inertia
3. m/s^2
4. Velocity
5. Friction
6. kg·m/s
7. Thrust

8. Gravity
9. Force
10. Forward
11. F = ma
12. 9.8 m/s^2
13. Friction
14. Elastic
15. Momentum
16. Gravitational
17. Uniform
18. Weight
19. Gravity
20. Action and Reaction

These answers correspond to the basic principles of force, motion, and laws of motion.

Here are 20 short answer questions based on Force and Laws of Motion for Class 9 CBSE:

1. What is force?
2. State Newton's First Law of Motion.
3. What is the SI unit of force?
4. What is the difference between mass and weight?
5. What is inertia?
6. Explain the concept of acceleration.
7. What is momentum?
8. State Newton's Second Law of Motion.
9. What is the relationship between force, mass, and acceleration?
10. What is the principle behind the working of a rocket?
11. How does friction affect motion?

12. State Newton's Third Law of Motion.
13. What is the law of conservation of momentum?
14. What is the difference between an elastic and inelastic collision?
15. What does the term 'apparent weight' mean?
16. What are contact forces? Give two examples.
17. What is the effect of unbalanced forces on a body?
18. What are action and reaction forces?
19. What is the effect of gravity on a falling object?
20. Why does an object in motion tend to stay in motion?

These questions are designed to assess your understanding of the fundamental concepts of force, motion, and laws of motion in a concise manner.

Here are some predictable questions that could come in the CBSE Class 9 Physics exam related to Force and Laws of Motion:

1. Define force. What are the effects of force?
2. State Newton's First Law of Motion. Explain with an example.
3. What is inertia? How is it related to Newton's First Law of Motion?
4. Explain Newton's Second Law of Motion. Derive the relation between force, mass, and acceleration.
5. A force of 10 N is applied to a body of mass 2 kg. What is the acceleration produced?
6. What is momentum? Derive the formula for momentum and explain its SI unit.
7. State and explain Newton's Third Law of Motion with an example.

8. What is the law of conservation of momentum? Explain with an example.
9. What are the different types of forces? Explain any two with examples.
10. What is the difference between mass and weight? Derive the relation between mass and weight.
11. Explain the effect of friction on motion. What are the factors that affect friction?
12. Define acceleration. A car increases its speed from 20 m/s to 30 m/s in 5 seconds. What is its acceleration?
13. What is the difference between uniform and non-uniform motion?
14. A ball of mass 0.5 kg is thrown upwards with a velocity of 10 m/s. What is the maximum height the ball will reach?
15. Explain the working of a rocket using Newton's Third Law of Motion.
16. What is the relation between force, mass, and acceleration according to Newton's Second Law?
17. What is the significance of the coefficient of friction?
18. In a collision between two objects, if the total momentum before and after the collision remains the same, what type of collision is it?
19. Explain how the action-reaction forces in Newton's Third Law do not cancel each other.
20. A body is moving with a uniform velocity. What can you conclude about the forces acting on it?

These questions cover a range of topics related to Force, Laws of Motion, Friction, and Momentum, which are important for the CBSE Class 9 Physics exam. It's essential to understand the core concepts and be ready to apply them in different situations.

Here are numerical questions based on Force and Laws of Motion for Class 9 CBSE Physics:

1. A car of mass 1000 kg is moving with an acceleration of 2 m/s^2. Calculate the force acting on the car.
2. A force of 5 N is applied on a body of mass 10 kg. What will be the acceleration of the body?
3. A ball of mass 0.2 kg is dropped from a height. What is its velocity just before hitting the ground? (Take g=9.8 m/s2g = 9.8 \, \text{m/s}^2 and the height as 10 m)
4. A body of mass 50 kg is moving with a velocity of 10 m/s. Calculate its momentum.
5. An object is subjected to a force of 20 N for 4 seconds. If the initial velocity of the object is 5 m/s, find the final velocity.
6. A 100 kg truck moves with an acceleration of 0.5 m/s^2. Calculate the force exerted by the engine of the truck.
7. A person of mass 60 kg is standing on a weighing scale in an elevator. If the elevator is accelerating upwards with 2 m/s^2, find the reading of the scale. (Take g=9.8 m/s2g = 9.8 \, \text{m/s}^2)
8. A ball is thrown vertically upwards with a velocity of 20 m/s. What is the time taken for it to reach the highest point?
9. A 50 kg person is standing in an elevator moving downward with an acceleration of 2 m/s^2. Find the apparent weight of the person. (Take g=9.8 m/s2g = 9.8 \, \text{m/s}^2)
10. A 10 kg object is acted upon by two forces: 15 N to the

east and 25 N to the west. Calculate the acceleration of the object.

11. A body of mass 5 kg is moving with a velocity of 12 m/s. Calculate its kinetic energy.
12. A rocket has a mass of 500 kg and expels gas at a rate of 50 kg/s. If the velocity of the expelled gas is 1500 m/s, calculate the thrust produced by the rocket.
13. A bullet of mass 0.01 kg is moving with a velocity of 400 m/s. Calculate its momentum.
14. A car of mass 800 kg is moving with a velocity of 36 km/h. Convert its velocity into m/s and calculate its momentum.
15. A force of 30 N is applied to a body of mass 12 kg. Calculate the acceleration produced in the body.
16. An object of mass 4 kg is moving with a velocity of 8 m/s. Find its momentum and kinetic energy.
17. A 1200 kg car is moving with a velocity of 30 m/s. What is the change in momentum when the car stops in 10 seconds?
18. A person pushes a box of mass 20 kg on a horizontal surface with a force of 100 N. If the frictional force is 40 N, calculate the acceleration of the box.
19. A stone is dropped from the top of a building. If it takes 5 seconds to hit the ground, calculate the height of the building. (Take g=9.8 m/s2g = 9.8 \, \text{m/s}^2)
20. A 3 kg object is moving with a velocity of 10 m/s. A force of 15 N is applied to stop it. How much time will it take to stop the object?

These numerical problems test your ability to apply the laws of motion, force, acceleration, and momentum to real-world scenarios.

Here are the answers without solutions to the numerical questions based on Force and Laws of Motion for Class 9 CBSE Physics:

1. 2000 N
2. 0.5 m/s^2
3. 14 m/s
4. 500 kg·m/s
5. 13 m/s
6. 50 N
7. 708 N
8. 2.04 seconds
9. 390 N
10. 1 m/s^2
11. 360 J
12. 75000 N
13. 4 kg·m/s
14. 8000 kg·m/s
15. 2.5 m/s^2
16. 32 kg·m/s, 128 J
17. -36000 kg·m/s
18. 3 m/s^2
19. 122.5 m
20. 2 seconds

These are the answers to the numerical questions.

Here are some tough numerical questions based on Force and Laws of Motion for Class 9 CBSE Physics:

1. A 500 kg car is moving at a velocity of 36 km/h. It suddenly comes to rest in 10 seconds due to the application of brakes. Calculate the force exerted by the brakes.

2. A rocket of mass 2000 kg is launching. The exhaust gases are ejected at a rate of 50 kg/s with a velocity of 1500 m/s. Calculate the thrust produced by the rocket.
3. A body of mass 3 kg is moving with an initial velocity of 5 m/s. A force of 15 N is applied in the direction of motion for 4 seconds. Calculate the final velocity of the body.
4. A 10 kg object is placed on a horizontal surface. The coefficient of friction between the surface and the object is 0.4. Calculate the frictional force acting on the object.
5. A stone is thrown vertically upward with a velocity of 30 m/s. Calculate the maximum height the stone will reach. (Take g=9.8 m/s2g = 9.8 \, \text{m/s}^2)
6. A 1000 kg truck is moving with a velocity of 20 m/s. Calculate the change in kinetic energy when the truck comes to rest in 5 seconds.
7. A 100 kg man is standing in an elevator. If the elevator accelerates upwards at 2 m/s^2, calculate the apparent weight of the man. (Take g=9.8 m/s2g = 9.8 \, \text{m/s}^2)
8. A 1200 kg car is moving at a velocity of 20 m/s. Calculate the force required to stop the car in 10 seconds.
9. A body of mass 15 kg is acted upon by a force of 50 N. Calculate the acceleration produced. If the body moves for 8 seconds, calculate the final velocity of the body.
10. A body of mass 12 kg is moving with a velocity of 5 m/s. Calculate its momentum. If the velocity is increased to 15 m/s, calculate the change in momentum.

These problems are designed to challenge your understanding of force, acceleration, momentum, and friction, and to test your ability to apply Newton's laws of motion in various scenarios.

Here are the answers to the tough numerical questions based on Force and Laws of Motion:

1. 1000 N
2. 75,000 N
3. 11 m/s
4. 40 N
5. 45.92 m
6. 200,000 J
7. 1200 N
8. 120,000 N
9. 3.33 m/s^2, 26.64 m/s
10. 180 kg·m/s, 180 kg·m/s

These are the final answers for the given numerical problems.

Numericals Based On Gravitation Chapter

Here are 20 Multiple Choice Questions (MCQs) based on the Gravitation chapter for Class 9 CBSE Physics.

1. Which of the following is the SI unit of gravitational force?

A) N·m

B) $N \cdot m^2/kg^2$

C) N

D) $kg \cdot m/s^2$

Answer: C) N

2. The gravitational force between two bodies depends on:

A) Their masses

B) The distance between their centers

C) Both the masses and the distance

D) None of the above

Answer: C) Both the masses and the distance

3. The value of acceleration due to gravity at the Earth's surface is approximately:

A) $9.8 m/s^2$

B) $10 m/s^2$

C) $0.98 m/s^2$

D) $1 m/s^2$

Answer: A) $9.8 m/s^2$

4. What is the gravitational force between two objects with masses of 5 kg and 10 kg, placed 2 meters apart? (Use G=6.674×10−11 N·m2/kg2G

A) 1.6685×10−10 N

B) 6.674×10−10 N

C) 3.337×10−10 N

D) 2.668×10−10 N

Answer: A) 1.6685×10−10 N

5. If the distance between two objects is doubled, the gravitational force between them becomes:

A) Half

B) One-fourth

C) Double

D) One-eighth

Answer: B) One-fourth

6. The escape velocity from the surface of the Earth is:

A) 7.9 km/s

B) 8.0 km/s

C) 11.2 km/s

D) 10.0 km/s

Answer: C) 11.2 km/s

7. The gravitational potential energy of an object of mass mm at height hh from the Earth's surface is given by:

A) U=mgh

B) U=GMmr

C) U=GMmh

D) U=mg

Answer: A) U=mgh

8. Which of the following is a characteristic of a gravitational field?

A) It is a vector quantity

B) It is a scalar quantity

C) It is dependent only on the mass of the object

D) It is a force field acting only on electrons

Answer: A) It is a vector quantity

9. The force of attraction between two bodies is directly proportional to:

A) The square of the distance between them
B) The mass of the bodies
C) The product of the masses of the bodies
D) The distance between them
Answer: C) The product of the masses of the bodies

10. The mass of an object does not change with:
A) Location
B) Height
C) Speed
D) None of the above
Answer: D) None of the above

11. The gravitational force acting on an object is called:
A) Normal force
B) Tension force
C) Weight
D) Frictional force
Answer: C) Weight

12. If the mass of the Earth were doubled, the value of gg would:
A) Double
B) Become half
C) Increase by four times
D) Stay the same
Answer: A) Double

13. The gravitational force on an object of mass mm is equal to:
A) m×gm \times g
B) m×Gm \times G
C) m2×gm^2 \times g
D) G×mG \times m
Answer: A) m×gm \times g

14. The gravitational force between two objects is 100 N. If the distance between them is halved, the new force

will be:

A) 200 N

B) 400 N

C) 50 N

D) 25 N

Answer: B) 400 N

15. Which of the following is true for a satellite orbiting the Earth?

A) The gravitational potential energy is positive.

B) The total mechanical energy is always zero.

C) The satellite never reaches escape velocity.

D) The satellite is in free fall.

Answer: D) The satellite is in free fall.

16. The force acting on a satellite orbiting Earth depends on:

A) The satellite's velocity

B) The radius of its orbit

C) The mass of the satellite

D) All of the above

Answer: D) All of the above

17. A planet moves faster in its orbit when it is:

A) Closer to the Sun

B) Farther from the Sun

C) In the same orbit

D) None of the above

Answer: A) Closer to the Sun

18. Which of the following is the escape velocity for the Moon?

A) 3.2 km/s

B) 2.4 km/s

C) 11.2 km/s

D) 0.8 km/s

Answer: B) 2.4 km/s

19. Kepler's second law of planetary motion is also known as:

A) Law of Ellipses

B) Law of Equal Areas

C) Harmonic Law

D) Law of Universal Gravitation

Answer: B) Law of Equal Areas

20. The escape velocity from a planet depends on:

A) The mass of the object

B) The radius of the planet

C) The acceleration due to gravity

D) Both B and C

Answer: D) Both B and C

Summary of Answers:

C) N

C) Both the masses and the distance

A) 9.8 m/s^2

A) 1.6685×10−10 N

B) One-fourth

C) 11.2 km/s

A) U=mghU = mgh

A) It is a vector quantity

C) The product of the masses of the bodies

D) None of the above

C) Weight

A) Double

A) m×gm \times g

B) 400 N

D) The satellite is in free fall.

D) All of the above

A) Closer to the Sun

B) 2.4 km/s

B) Law of Equal Areas

D) Both B and C

These MCQs cover a range of topics, from the basic concepts of gravitation to more advanced applications like escape velocity and Kepler's laws. They are designed to help students practice and solidify their understanding of the chapter.

Here are short answer questions based on the Gravitation chapter for Class 9 CBSE Physics:

1. What is gravitational force?

Answer:

Gravitational force is the force of attraction that pulls two objects toward each other due to their masses. It is one of the fundamental forces of nature and acts between all objects that have mass. The force is proportional to the product of the masses and inversely proportional to the square of the distance between their centers.

2. What is the value of acceleration due to gravity on the surface of the Earth?

Answer:

The value of acceleration due to gravity on the surface of the Earth is approximately 9.8 m/s29.8 \, \text{m/s}^2.

3. What is the difference between mass and weight?

Answer:

Mass: The amount of matter in an object, which remains constant regardless of location. Its SI unit is kilograms (kg).

Weight: The force exerted by gravity on an object. Weight varies with the location and is given by W=mgW = mg, where mm is the mass and gg is the acceleration due to gravity. Its SI unit is Newtons (N).

4. State Kepler's First Law of Planetary Motion.

Answer:

Kepler's First Law, also known as the Law of Ellipses, states that the orbit of every planet is an ellipse with the Sun at one of the two foci.

5. What is escape velocity?

Answer:

Escape velocity is the minimum speed an object must have in order to break free from the gravitational attraction of a planet or celestial body without further propulsion. For Earth, the escape velocity at the surface is approximately 11.2 km/s.

6. How does the gravitational force between two objects change when the distance between them is doubled?

Answer:

According to Newton's law of universal gravitation, the gravitational force between two objects is inversely proportional to the square of the distance between them. If the distance is doubled, the gravitational force becomes one-fourth of its original value.

7. Why does the value of gg vary at different places on Earth?

Answer:

The value of gg varies depending on altitude and latitude. It is slightly weaker at higher altitudes (since distance from the Earth's center increases) and at the equator due to the Earth's rotation (the Earth is slightly bulging at the equator). Therefore, the value of gg is slightly less at the equator and higher at the poles.

8. What is the gravitational potential energy of an object?

Answer:

Gravitational potential energy is the energy possessed by an object due to its position in a gravitational field. It is given by the formula U=mgh, where mm is the mass of the object, gg is the acceleration due to gravity, and hh is the height of the object above the reference point (usually the Earth's surface).

9. What is the relationship between gravitational force and the masses of the two objects?

Answer:

Gravitational force is directly proportional to the product of the masses of the two objects. That is, if the masses of the two objects increase, the gravitational force between them also increases. Mathematically, F∝m1m2r2, where m1m_1 and m2m_2 are the masses, and rr is the distance between them.

10. Why does an object fall towards the Earth when dropped?

Answer:

An object falls towards the Earth due to the gravitational force exerted by the Earth on the object. The Earth's mass creates a gravitational field, which attracts objects toward its center, causing them to fall when no other force is acting on them.

11. What is the value of acceleration due to gravity on the Moon?

Answer:

The value of acceleration due to gravity on the Moon is approximately 1.6 m/s2, which is about one-sixth of the value of gravity on Earth.

12. What is the formula for calculating the gravitational force between two objects?

Answer:

The formula for calculating the gravitational force between two objects is:

F=GMmr2

Where:

FF is the gravitational force,

GG is the universal gravitational constant (6.674×10−11 N·m2/kg2

M and m are the masses of the two objects,

r is the distance between the centers of the two objects.

13. What is the relation between the gravitational force and the distance between two objects?

Answer:

The gravitational force is inversely proportional to the square of the distance between the centers of the two objects. This means that if the distance between the objects doubles, the gravitational force becomes one-fourth of its original value.

14. What is the shape of the Earth's orbit around the Sun?

Answer:

The Earth's orbit around the Sun is an ellipse, with the Sun at one of the two foci. This is described by Kepler's First Law of Planetary Motion.

15. Why do astronauts feel weightless in space?

Answer:

Astronauts feel weightless in space because they are in a state of free fall. They are continuously falling towards Earth but moving forward at such a speed that the curvature of their path matches the curvature of the Earth. This creates the sensation of weightlessness, even though gravity is still acting on them.

16. How does the mass of an object affect its weight?

Answer:

The weight of an object is directly proportional to its mass. The greater the mass of an object, the greater its weight. Weight is given by the formula W=mgW = mg, where mm is the mass and gg is the acceleration due to gravity.

17. What is the significance of Kepler's Second Law of Planetary Motion?

Answer:

Kepler's Second Law, the Law of Equal Areas, states that a line joining a planet and the Sun sweeps out equal areas in equal intervals of time. This means that planets move faster when they are closer to the Sun and slower when they are farther away, maintaining the same area swept over time.

18. How does gravitational force act on a satellite in orbit around Earth?

Answer:

Gravitational force provides the necessary centripetal force that keeps a satellite in its orbit around the Earth. The satellite is constantly falling towards the Earth but moving forward at such a speed that it keeps missing the Earth, thus remaining in orbit.

19. What is the escape velocity from the Earth's surface?

Answer:

The escape velocity from the Earth's surface is approximately 11.2 km/s. This is the minimum velocity an object must have to break free from Earth's gravitational field without further propulsion.

20. How does the acceleration due to gravity vary with height above the Earth's surface?

Answer:

As height increases, the acceleration due to gravity decreases. This is because the distance from the Earth's center increases, reducing the gravitational force acting on an object. The relationship is given by the formula:

g′=g(1+hR)2

Where g′g′ is the acceleration due to gravity at height hh, gg is the acceleration due to gravity at the surface, and RR is the Earth's radius.

These short answer questions cover a wide range of topics from the Gravitation chapter and will help in understanding and reinforcing key concepts of the chapter for Class 9 CBSE Physics.

Here are numerical problems based on the Gravitation chapter for Class 9 CBSE Physics.

1. Gravitational Force between Two Objects

Given:

Mass of the Earth, M=6×1024 kg

Mass of an object, m=10 kg

Distance between the object and the center of the Earth, r=6.4×106 m

Find: The gravitational force acting on the object.

2. Gravitational Force between Two Objects at Different Distances

Given:

Mass of Earth, M=6×1024 kg

Mass of an object, m=20 kg

Distance between the Earth and the object is initially r=6.4×106 m

The distance is then increased to 2r.

Find:

(a) The initial gravitational force.

(b) The gravitational force when the distance is doubled.

3. Escape Velocity from the Earth

Given:

Mass of the Earth, M=6×1024 kg

Radius of the Earth, r=6.4×106 m

Find: The escape velocity from the Earth's surface.

4. Gravitational Potential Energy

Given:

Mass of the object, m=5 kg

Mass of the Earth, M=6×1024 kg

Distance from the center of the Earth, r=6.4×106 m

Find: The gravitational potential energy of the object.

5. Orbital Period of a Satellite

Given:

Mass of the Earth, M=6×1024 kg

Radius of the orbit of the satellite, r=4×107 m

Find: The orbital period of the satellite.

6. Weight of an Object on the Moon

Given:

Mass of the object, m=50 kg

Gravitational acceleration on the Moon, gMoon=1.6 m/s2

Find: The weight of the object on the Moon.

7. Gravitational Force between Two Satellites

Given:

Mass of satellite 1, m1=3000 kg

Mass of satellite 2, m2=5000 kg

Distance between the satellites, r=1500 km=1.5×106 m

Find: The gravitational force between the two satellites.

8. Gravitational Force on a 10 kg Object on Earth and Moon

Given:

Mass of the object, m=10 kg

Acceleration due to gravity on Earth, gEarth=9.8 m/s2

Acceleration due to gravity on the Moon, gMoon=1.6 m/s2

Find:

(a) The weight of the object on Earth.

(b) The weight of the object on the Moon.

9. Acceleration Due to Gravity at a Height Above Earth's Surface

Given:

Mass of the Earth, M=6×1024 kg

Radius of the Earth, r=6.4×106 m

Height above Earth's surface, h=1×106 m

Find: The value of acceleration due to gravity at this height.

10. Gravitational Force Acting on a Satellite in Orbit

Given:

Mass of the Earth, M=6×1024 kg

Mass of the satellite, m=1000 kg

Distance from the center of the Earth, r=4×107 m

Find: The gravitational force acting on the satellite.

Let me know if you'd like the solutions for these problems, and I'd be happy to provide them!

Numerical Based On Work Energy And Power

Here are 20 multiple-choice questions (MCQs) based on the topics of Work, Energy, and Power for Class 9 Physics (CBse):

1. What is the SI unit of work?

a) Newton

b) Joule

c) Watt

d) Meter

Answer: b) Joule

2. A force of 5 N is applied to an object, and it moves a distance of 2 meters. What is the work done?

a) 5 J

b) 2 J

c) 10 J

d) 7 J

Answer: c) 10 J

3. Work done is zero when:

a) The object is moving.

b) The force is perpendicular to the displacement.

c) The force is applied.

d) The object is at rest.

Answer: b) The force is perpendicular to the displacement.

4. What is the time period of a body in motion if it does 5 joules of work in 5 seconds?

a) 1 second

b) 5 seconds

c) 25 seconds

d) 10 seconds

Answer: b) 5 seconds

5. What is the formula for kinetic energy?

a) KE=12mv

b) KE=12mv2

c) KE=mv2

d) KE=mgh

Answer: b) KE=12mv2

6. The kinetic energy of an object depends on:

a) Its mass and velocity.

b) Its velocity and height.

c) Its mass and height.

d) Its speed and time.

Answer: a) Its mass and velocity.

7. A person does 100 J of work in 20 seconds. What is the power developed?

a) 5 W

b) 10 W

c) 15 W

d) 20 W

Answer: b) 5 W

8. What is the SI unit of power?

a) Joule

b) Watt

c) Newton

d) Meter per second

Answer: b) Watt

9. If the force applied on an object is in the direction of displacement, the work done is:

a) Negative

b) Zero

c) Positive

d) None of these

Answer: c) Positive

10. What is the potential energy of a body of mass 2 kg at a height of 10 m? (Take g=10 m/s2)

a) 20 J
b) 100 J
c) 200 J
d) 50 J

Answer: b) 100 J

11. If the velocity of an object is doubled, its kinetic energy becomes:

a) Half
b) Double
c) Four times
d) Ten times

Answer: c) Four times

12. Which of the following is not a form of energy?

a) Gravitational energy
b) Sound energy
c) Chemical energy
d) Pressure energy

Answer: d) Pressure energy

13. A body possesses maximum potential energy at:

a) The highest point of its motion.
b) The lowest point of its motion.
c) Any intermediate position.
d) None of these.

Answer: a) The highest point of its motion.

14. The energy possessed by a body due to its motion is called:

a) Gravitational energy
b) Kinetic energy
c) Thermal energy
d) Elastic energy

Answer: b) Kinetic energy

15. What happens to the kinetic energy of an object if its mass is doubled, but the velocity remains the same?

a) It remains unchanged.

b) It is halved.

c) It doubles.

d) It quadruples.

Answer: c) It doubles.

16. Which of the following statements is true about work?

a) Work is a vector quantity.

b) Work is done only when there is a displacement in the direction of the applied force.

c) Work and energy are independent quantities.

d) Work is not related to force.

Answer: b) Work is done only when there is a displacement in the direction of the applied force.

17. The energy required to lift a 1 kg object to a height of 1 meter is:

a) 10 J

b) 1 J

c) 100 J

d) 5 J

Answer: a) 10 J

18. What is the power of a machine that does 300 J of work in 60 seconds?

a) 2 W

b) 5 W

c) 10 W

d) 50 W

Answer: b) 5 W

19. Which of the following is a correct expression for the work-energy theorem?

a) Work done = Force × Displacement
b) Work done = Change in kinetic energy
c) Work done = Change in potential energy
d) Work done = Mass × Velocity

Answer: b) Work done = Change in kinetic energy

20. A body of mass 2 kg is moving with a velocity of 3 m/s. What is its kinetic energy?

a) 6 J
b) 9 J
c) 18 J
d) 36 J

Answer: b) 9 J

These 20 MCQs cover the key concepts related to Work, Energy, and Power, and are designed to help students prepare for their Class 9 CBSE Physics exams.

Here are 20 numerical problems based on the topics of Work, Energy, and Power for Class 9 CBSE Physics:

1. A force of 10 N is applied to a box, causing it to move a distance of 5 meters. Calculate the work done.

2. A car with a mass of 1000 kg is moving at a velocity of 20 m/s. Find its kinetic energy.

3. A person lifts a 50 kg box to a height of 2 meters. Calculate the potential energy of the box. (Take g=9.8 m/s2g = 9.8 \, \text{m/s}^2)

4. A machine does 200 J of work in 10 seconds. What is the power of the machine?

5. A body of mass 5 kg is moving with a velocity of 4 m/s. Find its kinetic energy.

6. A force of 12 N is applied on an object and moves it 8 meters. Calculate the work done if the angle between the

force and displacement is 0°.

7. A car is moving with a speed of 30 m/s and has a mass of 800 kg. Find the total kinetic energy of the car.

8. A ball of mass 0.5 kg is thrown upwards with an initial velocity of 10 m/s. Calculate its kinetic energy just after being thrown.

9. A spring is compressed by 0.2 meters. The spring constant is 200 N/m. Calculate the elastic potential energy stored in the spring.

10. A person lifts a weight of 40 kg through a height of 3 meters. Calculate the work done.

11. A machine consumes 5000 J of energy in 5 minutes. What is the power used by the machine?

12. A bullet of mass 10 g is fired with a speed of 500 m/s. Calculate its kinetic energy.

13. A boy lifts a 20 kg box to a height of 5 meters. Calculate the potential energy gained by the box. (Take g=9.8 m/s2g = 9.8 \, \text{m/s}^2)

14. A motor does 1200 J of work in 4 seconds. What is the power output of the motor?

15. A cyclist is moving with a speed of 12 m/s. If his mass is 60 kg, calculate his kinetic energy.

16. A force of 15 N is applied to move a box 4 meters. If the force acts at an angle of 30°, calculate the work done.

17. A 10 kg object is dropped from a height of 20 meters. Calculate its potential energy just before it hits the ground. (Take g=9.8 m/s2g = 9.8 \, \text{m/s}^2)

18. A body of mass 2 kg is at rest. After 5 seconds, its velocity becomes 10 m/s. Calculate the work done on the body.

19. A machine operates at 60% efficiency. If the input energy is 2000 J, what is the useful work done by the machine?

20. An athlete runs 100 meters in 12 seconds. Calculate the power developed by the athlete if the total work done is 1200 J.

These are 20 numerical problems that will help in understanding the concepts of Work, Energy, and Power. They involve different aspects of these topics, such as calculating work, kinetic energy, potential energy, and power, and are designed for Class 9 students.

Here are the one-word answers for the 20 numerical problems based on Work, Energy, and Power:

1. 50 J
2. 200,000 J
3. 980 J
4. 20 W
5. 40 J
6. 96 J
7. 360,000 J
8. 25 J
9. 4 J
10. 1,176 J
11. 16.67 W
12. 1250 J
13. 980 J
14. 300 W
15. 4,320 J
16. 60 J
17. 1960 J
18. 100 J
19. 1200 J
20. 100 W

These answers correspond to the numerical questions provided earlier. Each represents the calculated value for the respective problem.

Here are 20 more challenging numerical problems based on Work, Energy, and Power for Class 9 CBSE Physics:

1. A 2 kg object is moving at a velocity of 10 m/s. Calculate its kinetic energy. After that, the velocity is doubled. Find the new kinetic energy.

2. A 50 kg object is lifted to a height of 8 meters. Calculate the potential energy. Afterward, it is lifted by an additional 5 meters. What is the new potential energy?

3. A car with a mass of 1200 kg accelerates from 0 to 30 m/s in 15 seconds. Calculate the work done to accelerate the car.

4. A machine lifts a 30 kg object through a height of 6 meters in 4 seconds. Calculate the power required.

5. A person applies a force of 40 N to push a box 10 meters along a horizontal surface. If the angle between the force and displacement is 30°, calculate the work done.

6. A ball of mass 0.3 kg is thrown vertically upwards with an initial velocity of 20 m/s. How high will it rise before its kinetic energy is completely converted to potential energy?

7. A spring with a spring constant of 250 N/m is stretched by 0.5 meters. Calculate the potential energy stored in the spring.

8. A body of mass 4 kg is moving with a velocity of 15 m/s. Calculate its kinetic energy. If the velocity is reduced to 10 m/s, what is the new kinetic energy?

9. A 1000 kg car moves with a speed of 15 m/s. Calculate the work done by the car if its speed is increased to 25 m/s.

10. A 10 kg mass is raised to a height of 12 meters. Calculate the work done. Afterward, the object is raised by another 3 meters. What is the new work done?

11. A cyclist accelerates from 5 m/s to 15 m/s in 10 seconds. If the mass of the cyclist and bike is 80 kg, calculate the work done during the acceleration.

12. A person does 500 J of work to lift a 25 kg weight. How high has the weight been lifted?

13. A body of mass 3 kg is moving with a velocity of 6 m/s. Calculate the work done to stop the body by applying a constant force.

14. A 5 kg object is pushed with a force of 50 N over a distance of 8 meters. If the force is applied at an angle of 60° to the surface, calculate the work done.

15. A power station generates 2 MW of power. How much energy is generated in 10 minutes?

16. A body of mass 3 kg is dropped from a height of 50 meters. Calculate the speed of the body just before it hits the ground. (Assume no air resistance and g=9.8 m/s2g = 9.8 \, \text{m/s}^2)

17. A person does 150 J of work in 15 seconds. Calculate the power developed. Afterward, the work is doubled, but the time is halved. What is the new power?

18. A 20 kg object is thrown vertically upwards with an initial velocity of 15 m/s. Calculate the maximum height it will reach. (Take g=10 m/s2g = 10 \, \text{m/s}^2)

19. A force of 200 N is applied to a car that moves at a constant velocity of 5 m/s. Calculate the power delivered by the car.

20. A 3 kg object is moving with a velocity of 12 m/s. If the object is brought to rest by applying a constant force, calculate the work done by the force in bringing the object to rest.

These problems involve more complex scenarios, where concepts of kinetic energy, potential energy, work, and power are applied in various contexts. They are meant to help students better understand the intricacies of energy and force interactions.

Here are the one-word answers for the 20 difficult numerical problems based on Work, Energy, and Power:

1. 500 J, 2000 J
2. 3920 J, 4900 J
3. 540,000 J
4. 180 W
5. 346.41 J
6. 20 m
7. 31.25 J
8. 900 J, 600 J
9. 1,500,000 J
10. 1440 J, 1800 J
11. 4800 J
12. 2 meters
13. 54 J
14. 200 J
15. 1,200,000 J
16. 31.3 m/s
17. 10 W, 40 W
18. 11.25 m
19. 1000 W
20. 432 J

These answers correspond to the respective numerical problems listed earlier. Each answer provides the calculated result for the given problem.

Numerical Based On Sound Chapter

Here are 20 multiple-choice questions (MCQs) based on the Sound Chapter from Class 9 CBSE:

1. The speed of sound in air is:

a) 1500 m/s
b) 343 m/s
c) 500 m/s
d) 123 m/s

Answer: b) 343 m/s

2. The frequency of a sound wave is measured in:

a) Hertz
b) Decibels
c) Meters
d) Joules

Answer: a) Hertz

3. Which of the following is the unit of sound intensity?

a) Watt per meter square
b) Decibel
c) Hertz
d) Newton

Answer: a) Watt per meter square

4. What is the time period of a wave with a frequency of 10 Hz?

a) 10 seconds
b) 1 second
c) 0.1 seconds
d) 0.01 seconds

Answer: b) 1 second

5. The phenomenon of sound traveling faster in warmer air than in cooler air is called:

a) Refraction

b) Diffraction

c) Reflection

d) Speed variation with temperature

Answer: d) Speed variation with temperature

6. The wavelength of a sound wave is the distance between:

a) Two consecutive rarefactions

b) Two consecutive compressions

c) One compression and one rarefaction

d) Both b and c

Answer: d) Both b and c

7. The loudness of sound is measured in:

a) Hertz

b) Decibels

c) Meters

d) Joules

Answer: b) Decibels

8. The unit of frequency is:

a) Hertz

b) Decibel

c) Newton

d) Watt

Answer: a) Hertz

9. Sound waves are:

a) Longitudinal

b) Transverse

c) Both

d) None of the above

Answer: a) Longitudinal

10. Which of the following factors does not affect the speed of sound?

a) Temperature

b) Pressure

c) Medium

d) Humidity

Answer: b) Pressure

11. The frequency of a sound wave is 1000 Hz. What is its time period?

a) 0.01 seconds

b) 0.1 seconds

c) 0.001 seconds

d) 1 second

Answer: a) 0.01 seconds

12. The phenomenon where sound bends around obstacles is called:

a) Reflection

b) Diffraction

c) Refraction

d) Echo

Answer: b) Diffraction

13. Which of the following is not a property of sound waves?

a) They need a medium to propagate

b) They travel faster in gases than in solids

c) They are longitudinal waves

d) They carry energy

Answer: b) They travel faster in gases than in solids

14. The sound waves with frequencies less than 20 Hz are called:

a) Audible sound

b) Infrasonic

c) Ultrasonic

d) Subsonic

Answer: b) Infrasonic

15. If the frequency of a sound wave is increased, the wavelength will:

a) Increase

b) Decrease

c) Stay the same

d) Become zero

Answer: b) Decrease

16. The sound travels fastest in:

a) Air

b) Water

c) Steel

d) Vacuum

Answer: c) Steel

17. Which of the following does not produce sound?

a) Vibrating body

b) Static body

c) Moving body

d) Disturbing medium

Answer: b) Static body

18. In which medium does sound travel the slowest?

a) Air

b) Water

c) Steel

d) Vacuum

Answer: a) Air

19. The speed of sound in air at 0°C is:

a) 320 m/s

b) 343 m/s

c) 300 m/s

d) 255 m/s

Answer: a) 320 m/s

20. The Doppler effect is observed when there is a change in:

a) Frequency
b) Amplitude
c) Wavelength
d) All of the above

Answer: a) Frequency

These questions are designed to assess your understanding of the basic concepts related to sound waves, their properties, and behavior in different media. They also touch upon key principles like frequency, wavelength, speed, and the Doppler effect.

Here are 20 short answer type questions based on the Sound Chapter from Class 9 CBSE:

1. What is sound?

Answer: Sound is a form of energy that produces a sensation of hearing. It is produced by the vibration of objects and travels through a medium (solid, liquid, or gas).

2. How does sound travel?

Answer: Sound travels as longitudinal waves, where particles of the medium vibrate in the direction of wave propagation. These vibrations cause compressions and rarefactions.

3. What is the speed of sound in air at 20°C?

Answer: The speed of sound in air at 20°C is approximately 343 meters per second.

4. What is the relationship between frequency and wavelength?

Answer: The frequency and wavelength of a sound wave are inversely related. As the frequency increases, the wavelength decreases, and vice versa. This relationship is given by the formula v=f×λ, where vv is the speed of sound, ff is the frequency, and λ\lambda is the wavelength.

5. Define amplitude in terms of sound.

Answer: Amplitude refers to the maximum displacement of particles from their equilibrium position in a sound wave. It determines the loudness or intensity of the sound.

6. What is the unit of frequency?

Answer: The unit of frequency is Hertz (Hz), which represents one vibration per second.

7. What is the time period of a wave?

Answer: The time period is the time taken by a particle to complete one full vibration. It is the reciprocal of frequency and is measured in seconds.

8. What is the Doppler effect?

Answer: The Doppler effect is the change in frequency or wavelength of a sound wave due to the relative motion between the source of sound and the observer.

9. Why is sound unable to travel through a vacuum?

Answer: Sound requires a medium (solid, liquid, or gas) to propagate, as it relies on the vibration of particles. In a vacuum, there are no particles to transmit the sound waves.

10. What is the effect of temperature on the speed of sound?

Answer: The speed of sound increases with an increase in temperature because warmer air has more energetic particles that transmit sound waves more efficiently.

11. What is the unit of sound intensity?

Answer: The unit of sound intensity is Watt per meter squared (W/m^2).

12. What is an echo?

Answer: An echo is the reflection of sound waves off a surface, such as a wall or mountain, and returning to the listener after a delay.

13. What is the difference between pitch and loudness?

Answer: Pitch refers to the frequency of a sound, determining whether it is high or low, while loudness refers to the amplitude of the sound wave, determining the sound's intensity or volume.

14. Define wavelength in sound.

Answer: Wavelength is the distance between two consecutive points in phase, such as two consecutive compressions or rarefactions, in a sound wave.

15. Why do we hear sound more clearly in solids than in air?

Answer: Sound travels faster and more efficiently in solids because the particles are closely packed, allowing quicker transmission of vibrations compared to air, where particles are more spread out.

16. What is a longitudinal wave?

Answer: A longitudinal wave is a wave in which the particle displacement is parallel to the direction of wave propagation, as seen in sound waves.

17. What is the range of human hearing?

Answer: The range of human hearing is generally from 20 Hz to 20,000 Hz.

18. What are infrasonic and ultrasonic waves?

Answer: Infrasonic waves have frequencies below 20 Hz, while ultrasonic waves have frequencies above 20,000 Hz. Both are beyond the range of human hearing.

19. What is the effect of pressure on the speed of sound?

Answer: In general, pressure has a negligible effect on the speed of sound. However, the medium's density and temperature have a more significant impact on sound speed.

20. Why do we hear sound vibrations in a medium but not in a vacuum?

Answer: In a medium, sound vibrations cause particles to move, transmitting the energy of sound waves. In a vacuum, there are no particles to vibrate and carry the sound, so sound cannot travel.

These short-answer questions help assess understanding of the key concepts related to sound waves, their properties, and behavior.

Here are 20 numerical problems based on the Sound Chapter from Class 9 CBSE. These questions will help you practice concepts such as the speed of sound, frequency, wavelength, time period, and the Doppler effect.

1. The speed of sound in air is 340 m/s. How long will it take for sound to travel 1020 meters?

2. A tuning fork produces a sound with a frequency of 512 Hz. What is the time period of the sound?

3. The frequency of a sound wave is 256 Hz. What is its wavelength if the speed of sound in air is 340 m/s?

4. A person is standing 500 meters away from a reflecting surface. How much time will it take for the echo to return?

5. If a sound wave has a frequency of 500 Hz and a wavelength of 0.68 meters, what is the speed of sound?

6. A sound wave has a frequency of 1200 Hz. What is its time period?

7. The speed of sound in water is 1500 m/s. How much time will sound take to travel 4500 meters in water?

8. A sound wave travels through air at 343 m/s. What is the wavelength if its frequency is 1000 Hz?

9. A police car is moving at 30 m/s towards a stationary observer. The frequency of the siren is 1200 Hz, and the speed of sound is 340 m/s. What is the frequency heard by the observer?

10. A bat emits ultrasonic sound at a frequency of 50,000 Hz. What is the time period of the sound wave?

11. The distance between a person and the mountain is 800 meters. If the speed of sound in air is 340 m/s, how much time does the echo take to return?

12. A sound wave with a frequency of 400 Hz travels in air with a speed of 330 m/s. What is the wavelength of the wave?

13. A sound source is moving at a speed of 50 m/s and is emitting sound waves with a frequency of 2000 Hz. What is the wavelength of the sound waves?

14. The frequency of a sound wave is 600 Hz. Calculate the wavelength of the sound if the speed of sound is 343 m/s.

15. A person hears a sound of frequency 800 Hz when the source is at rest. If the source moves towards the observer with a speed of 20 m/s, what will be the observed frequency? (Speed of sound = 343 m/s)

16. The time period of a wave is 0.0025 seconds. What is its frequency?

17. A sound wave with a frequency of 150 Hz travels through a medium. If the speed of sound in the medium is 450 m/s, what is the wavelength?

18. A sound wave travels through a medium with a speed of 350 m/s. If the wavelength is 0.5 meters, what is the frequency of the sound wave?

19. The speed of sound in a medium is 330 m/s. What is the time taken by the sound to travel 990 meters?

20. A wave has a frequency of 10,000 Hz and travels with a speed of 343 m/s. What is the wavelength of the wave?

These problems cover key concepts of sound such as speed, frequency, wavelength, time period, and Doppler effect, and they will help reinforce the understanding of these topics.

Answers

1. 3 seconds
2. 0.00195 seconds
3. 1.328 meters
4. 2.94 seconds
5. 340 m/s
6. 0.000833 seconds
7. 3 seconds
8. 0.343 meters
9. 1311 Hz
10. 0.00002 seconds
11. 4.71 seconds
12. 0.825 meters
13. 0.025 meters
14. 0.571 meters
15. 850.46 Hz
16. 400 Hz
17. 3 meters
18. 700 Hz

19. 3 seconds
20. 0.0343 meters

These are the concise answers to each question in the numerical set.

www.ingramcontent.com/pod-product-compliance
Lightning Source LLC
LaVergne TN
LVHW041022150826
845672LV00001B/173

* 9 7 9 8 8 9 6 9 9 0 8 4 0 *